CAREFUL ECONOMICS

Careful Economics

Integrating Caring Activities and Economic Science

by

Maren A. Jochimsen

KLUWER ACADEMIC PUBLISHERS
BOSTON / DORDRECHT / LONDON

A C.I.P. Catalogue record for this book is available from the Library of Congress.

ISBN 1-4020-7467-0

Published by Kluwer Academic Publishers,
P.O. Box 17, 3300 AA Dordrecht, The Netherlands.

Sold and distributed in North, Central and South America
by Kluwer Academic Publishers,
101 Philip Drive, Norwell, MA 02061, U.S.A.

In all other countries, sold and distributed
by Kluwer Academic Publishers,
P.O. Box 322, 3300 AH Dordrecht, The Netherlands.

Cover: Jasper Jochimsen and Armin Behles, Berlin

Printed on acid-free paper

Printed in the Netherlands.

To Margarethe and Reimut Jochimsen

TABLE OF CONTENTS

PREFACE

Much like their authors, the ideas behind books can grow and change on the way from proposal to manuscript. I originally planned to join the discussion on care and economics at a different, more policy-oriented level, hoping to identify the conditions under which caring services are taken to the market. In approaching the task, however, I realized that economic science lacked an overall concept of caring. Economists' notions of caring and their knowledge of its basic elements and structural characteristics were fragmented. Caring activities were treated in the context of household work, unpaid work, or subsistence and informal work. None of the different approaches shared a common frame of reference. This has made it impossible to study caring activities *across* the various realms of the economy, independent of whether provided in a family setting, purchased on the market, or supplied by the state or society. I therefore found I had to begin my questioning earlier, at the level of basic understandings and concepts.

How can the characteristics of caring be described in economic theory? What concepts and analytical tools are needed to adequately describe and analyze a caring situation in economics? What existing economic concepts may be applied, what new concepts have to be introduced or developed? What is the structure of the realm of care, often enough hidden from and invisible to the eyes of conventional economic theory?

In examining these questions, in *conceptualizing* caring for economic theory, I took as my test case caring for dependents: children, the elderly, the sick, and the disabled. This involved the theoretical treatment of dependency caring's central characteristics. But standard assumptions of economic theory soon reached their analytical boundaries in the attempt to perform this task. For the autonomy, symmetry, and independence conventionally regarded as the standard characteristics of economic exchanges are rarely found in caring for dependents, whose distinguishing features, by contrast, are limited autonomy, asymmetry, dependency, and non-market structures. These characteristics can only be treated with their own set of analytical tools. To do so, a differentiated or *careful economic* perspective must be adopted, one that is sensitive to and reflective of the caring situations it seeks to understand.

In my effort to uncover the structure of caring situations, systematize its elements, and integrate current approaches to caring, another important dimension revealed itself: the otherwise hidden explanatory faculty of concepts such as asymmetry, dependency, and limited autonomy, and their relevance for the social and economic organization of caring. The asymmetric, for example, has a formative power of its own, and the central analytical categories of caring also provide us with the basic coordinates for socially and economically addressing caring needs.

The arguments I will outline move at the conceptual level. A key idea behind the work is that such a conceptualization of caring is essential for appropriate policy analysis. Only with a more careful, deeper understanding of caring, only after putting together a concept of its structural characteristics and the driving forces behind it, can we constructively evaluate the impact of public policy on the caring sector and develop policies to deal with its present crisis. *Careful economics* is therefore a theoretical challenge of highly practical relevance.

ACKNOWLEDGEMENTS

Many people and institutions have contributed to the development of ideas outlined in this book. The international research was funded by the Swiss National Science Foundation under Awards No. 81SG-044358 and No. 8210-46573 and was begun at the University of St. Gallen with the encouragement of Werner Wunderlich. Heinz Hauser and Gebhard Kirchgässner supported my grant applications and provided comments at various stages of the project and first drafts of the manuscript.

Three university communities hosted me in the formative process. By opening up the possibilities of research, discussion, and learning, they have had a decisive impact on my work. Geoffrey Hodgson, the Judge Institute for Management Studies at the University of Cambridge (1995-1996), his doctoral students, and the members of Tony Lawson's Workshop on Realism and Economics gave me the chance to develop and discuss the initial ideas of my project. Juliet Schor, the Committee for Womens' Studies, and the Economics Department of Harvard University (1996-1998) invited me to join their discussions. Stephen Marglin, the participants of Harvard's Political Economy Seminar, and Lucie White from Harvard Law School commented on early papers. The directors and fellows of the Radcliffe Public Policy Institute and the Bunting Institute at Harvard University challenged me with ever new questions and fresh elaborations on related topics. I owe specific thanks to Julie Nelson for her encouragement, valuable comments, and helpful suggestions as the project developed. Siv Gustafsson, Edith Kuiper, and the Department of Economics and Econometrics of the Universiteit van Amsterdam (1998-1999) introduced me to the Dutch community of care researchers, and gave me the opportunity to present and discuss my work. I received valuable comments from Selma Sevenhuijsen, Jeanne de Brujin, Janneke Plantenga, and members of the *Feminist Economics Network in the Netherlands (FENN)*, especially Irene van Staveren and Margreth Hoek. Special thanks go to Edith Kuiper for her invaluable support, friendship, memorable discussions, and common projects.

I also benefited greatly from the sharing of ideas at several seminars and conferences where I have presented my work, including the Political Economy Seminar at Harvard University (1998), the Belle van Zuylen Institute in Amsterdam (1998), the Gender and Economics Seminar at the University of Amsterdam (1999), the Annual Conference of the *European Association for Evolutionary Political Economy (EAEPE)* in Prague (1999), the Annual Conference of *The Society for the Advancement of Socio-Economics (SASE)* in London (2000), and the Annual Conference of the

Institute of Institutional and Social-Economics (iise) at the University of Bremen (2001).

Susan Himmelweit provided helpful comments at formative stages of my approach. Karin Peschel, Udo Ernst Simonis, and Renate Schubert commented on early portions of the work. Adelheid Biesecker was kind enough to read and comment in detail on the draft manuscript. The founding members of the *International Association for Feminist Economics (IAFFE) Europe* and the *Netzwerk Vorsorgendes Wirtschaften* (Network Caring Economy) gave me the confidence that this was a valuable project. Stefan Weidle gave me valuable pointers for publishing the work. Albert Brancato read the manuscript with the eyes and mind of a native speaker; his suggestions and our discussions have improved its clarity.

Among my friends, special thanks go to Margarita M. Balmaceda for her continuous encouragement, suggestions, and ongoing active support. Ulrike Knobloch accompanied the naissance of the book from its very beginning, always ready to encourage, read, criticize, suggest, and sympathize. Our early common papers marked the start and in many ways laid the foundations for what is elaborated here.

My family has been a great source of support and warmest caring during research and writing. I am grateful to Ida Stammel and Frieda and Bill Braun for giving me a home West of the Atlantic. I owe special thanks to Ilse Müller, Jasper Jochimsen, and Sabine Belz for their help and, together with Mira and Ada, for always being there.

To my great sorrow, one of the strongest supporters of this project did not live to witness its materialization as a book: my father set an example by his own scientific curiosity and uncompromising attention to questions he deemed important, even when they were unpopular with the established scientific community. He read and commented on initial sections of the project, helped influence its direction, encouraged its pursuit against all odds, and never doubted its completion. My mother has given me strength by her own undaunted courage and her originality, creativity, and persistence in her work. Always ready to listen and discuss, she provided invaluable suggestions and active caring support, and helped me persevere through the project's most difficult times. To my parents I dedicate this book.

I

DIRECTIONS FOR ANALYSIS

Part I introduces the topic. It first outlines the importance of caring as a subject for economic theory and explains the aim and structure of the book. The task of integrating caring activities and economic theory is then defined and the cornerstones of the analysis are described.

Chapter 1

AIM AND SCOPE OF THE WORK

Sketching the ground

To care is to relate: to fellow human beings, to the environment, to the self, as individuals and members of society, consciously, existentially, and over time. Caring activities, especially child care, care for the elderly, and care for the sick and disabled, are central and integral parts of human existence. Their effective and adequate provision is a precondition for all other human undertakings, which ultimately rely on and are interwoven with caring activities. Individual competence to care is a challenge to our own humanity. But providing efficient and appropriate care to those members of society who need it is an increasingly complex task for postindustrial service economies – both empirically and theoretically.

As economies move away from their traditional agricultural and manufacturing bases and adopt advanced industrial and service structures, they are characterized by ongoing rationalization, growing commercialization, and the fulfillment of an increasing number of needs by modern information and communication technologies. This radically alters economic and social relations as well as individuals' personal outlooks on life. These ever evolving trends coincide with important changes in the need for the provision of caring activities and include phenomena such as aging populations, changing family patterns, gains in female employment, and the stratification of employment and income. Society and policy makers are thus faced with the constant challenge of sustaining the level and quality of caring activities.

In today's Western culture, however, caring activities and those who perform them operate in what would seem to be an "invisible universe," their economic and social contributions hidden from official sight. And this might even be getting worse, the potential result being a withering of many of the very roots of civil conduct and the human basis for a dignified and worthy life. Our failure to keep sight of the "caring universe," however, comes at a cost. For the invisible is still an item of use. Just as is the case with the natural environment, the invisible realm of care is subject to the costs unconsciously and unintentionally imposed on it by the economic system. This may lead to the point where the roots and workings of highly developed market economies may overextend themselves in the long-term, accelerating an already evident decline in values associated with this trend.

In the present-day context of economic development and the social evolution of personal and human needs, caring activities and their appropriate social and economic provision confront us with urgent questions. Responding to these questions requires careful analysis. Issues connected with the provision of caring services involve both individual lives and overall economic policy. Measures applied in the context of fiscal, family, labor-market, corporate, and educational policies, even if most are not specifically care-oriented, still have an impact on the provision of caring activities in society. They do so by assigning, or not assigning, material and financial resources, labor, time, and skills to caring activities. Finding the right response to the issues at stake is a challenge to be met by individuals and policy makers alike. In all likelihood, this challenge, which focuses on the social and economic organization of the adequate provision of caring activities in market economies, will become more pressing and comprehensive as time goes on.

But how are the tasks of optimally securing the necessary caring services to be tackled? How can the impact of policies on the provision of caring activities, how can policies' contribution to this provision be evaluated? What is the theoretical ground for designing such policies? These questions are of growing importance. The situation not only involves practical and political challenges; it also poses theoretical challenges to the sciences involved, one of them being economics.

The importance of caring as a subject for economic theorizing

The performance of caring activities and provision of caring services constitute one of the main pillars supporting every society and economic system; their effective rendering is a precondition for all other economic activities. Without appropriate child care, care for the sick and disabled, and care for the elderly, no economic system could function in the long run since adult workers could not be raised and educated; nor could they return to the work place after illness, or be gainfully active if having to care for their elders. Activities of regeneration and caring services are processes that render possible the functioning of economies. (Jochimsen and Knobloch 1993, 1997)

Care, however, has not yet become a central category of economic and social analysis. Caring activities are usually studied in the context of their often dominant, institutional realm of providing (e.g. household work), following what is perceived as some of their eminent characteristics (e.g. unpaid work), or within theoretical approaches that treat issues outside formal (taxed) market coordination that are organized and pecuniary (e.g. forms of subsistence work or informal work). Until recently, standard economics knew comparatively little about caring activities and their contribution to the functioning of the economy and society as a whole. Economic theory took their performance for granted. Caring activities were, and largely still are, considered *pre- or post-economic* activities. As a consequence of this blindness toward the real importance and contribution of caring to the functioning of economic systems, standard economic theory is unable to represent the context of reproduction (replenishment and regeneration) which is so essential to human beings. (cf. also Benería 1999; Himmelweit 2002)

Because the pervasiveness and key significance of caring in terms of human and social life is not appreciated, the activities of those who give care tend to be further marginalized. The virtual lack of valuing care in its status as largely unpaid work, and its location within the private and the emotional spheres, pushes any understanding of care's broader social, moral, economic, and political ramifications into fields that are difficult to handle. A dualistic understanding of the functioning of economies, which distinguishes the fully integrated, efficiently organized world of production, exchange, and (hedonistic) consumption from the world of subsistence, leads to a consideration of care work, which is (still) predominantly unpaid, as part of the informal economy with little or no visibility or significance. Although care and its component parts are increasingly discussed within the context of industrial societies, they are not yet considered as a comprehensive issue and regarded in a systematic manner. But, as is becoming dramatically apparent with regard to the situation in the welfare sector today: without a profound understanding of caring activities, societal welfare cannot be reasonably theorized and politically shaped.

The conviction behind this study is that, in view of the importance of caring activities in responding to the *condition humaine* and their fundamental significance for the functioning of economic and social systems, we can ill afford to marginalize them. Up to now, marginalization has increasingly occurred in the course of societal evolution in the ever more sophisticated structures of the division of labor based on commercialization and, perhaps even more regrettable, in the artificially limited scope of theoretical analysis. The invisible universe has a structure. And a more comprehensive understanding of it is needed.

In general economics, the practical understanding and systematic application of a theoretical framework for evaluating caring activities are still rather fragmented. The theoretical approaches that have been suggested, predominantly by feminist economists, must be brought together and integrated into an overall concept. Without a systematic conceptualization of caring in economics, without defining, treating, and analyzing caring and its social and economic organization, opportunities for acquiring a thorough view of the present and an outlook for the future of providing caring activities will be lost.

Aim of the book

The work's focus is conceptual. Its hypothesis is that to formulate, evaluate, and shape care policies we need to understand the basic structure in which caring activities are provided – in the personal and private realm, the market, the state sector, and civil society. By considering various theoretical constructs and drafting a coherent concept as a frame of reference, we can more adequately treat the unresolved questions.

The work seeks to uncover the structure of the invisible and the ignored, and to propose a systematic conceptualization identifying and explaining the function of the main features of caring activities. The assumption is that certain distinctive features common to all caring activities – whether paid or unpaid; whether provided in the domestic sphere, in a civic context, in the market, or as part of a state welfare system; whether performed by women or men; whether undertaken in the formal or the informal economy – may be understood and analyzed using the *concept of an effective caring situation* as a common frame of reference. This concept aptly covers the effective provision of caring activities before and beyond their institutional arrangements, i.e. *pre-institutionally*, and thus furnishes a frame of reference for the study of the social organization of caring situations.

For the systematic integration of caring activities into economic theory, attention must be paid to the analytical tools and concepts inherently connected to caring situations. A structure unites the characteristics of caring situations and provides points of coordination for their social and economic organization. Our study suggests that the economic analysis of caring should start from and evolve around the basic structure of caring situations – comprising motivation, work, and resource components – and that concepts of limited choice, asymmetry, and dependency should be added to the package already comprising the conventional tools of freedom of choice, symmetry, and independence.

The systematic conceptualization of caring activities is a prerequisite for any study of the social organization of caring activities *across* the economy, whether these activities are provided in the latter's formal or informal part. It enables analysis of the effectiveness of the provision of caring activities within a specific domain of the economy, as well as a comparison of the provision of caring activities within or between different domains. The impact on the provision of caring activities as the result of different modes of coordination in the market and non-market economies may thus be studied. Tackling these questions is of key importance for understanding the present critical state in the provision of caring activities as well as for identifying starting points for appropriate solutions.

The aim is to open up and inform the established science of the hidden explanatory value offered by the comprehensive conceptualization of caring situations, and to help move the questions surrounding the study of caring and the social organization of caring situations from the level of pre/post-economic activities (regarded as not having any theoretical impact on economic theory) to the plane of decisive theoretical and practical importance that they deserve.

Structure of the book

The argument will proceed in three main steps:

Part I develops the analytical frame of reference for the investigation. Caring activities affecting persons (caring for others as well as self-care) and their essential characteristics are presented as the object of investigation. Caring for dependents (child care, elder care, and care for the sick and the disabled) is identified as the major bottleneck in the provision of caring activities as well as in the theoretical conceptualization of caring activities. For these reasons, caring situations for dependents are taken as the starting point and continuous point of reference for the further conceptual development and analysis. The integration of these caring situations into economic thought means conceptualizing a situation of human interaction that is different from our typical exchange situation. It requires certain basic assumptions differing from the common assumptions that the economy operates on the basis of autonomous and independent economic agents in full command of their physical and mental capabilities and equally free to choose market entry or exit. Situations of caring for dependents, however, are characterized by relatedness of the individuals involved, by asymmetric starting positions, by varying degrees of dependency of the individuals, and by a certain asymmetric power structure underlying the provision of caring services for dependents. (Chapter 2)

Part II of our study focuses on the search for an adequate concept for caring that can include caring for dependents. Basic conceptual approaches to caring in economics will be examined to see whether and how they incorporate or are able to conceptualize caring for dependents. These include: conceptualization of caring within the preference-based, utility-oriented, economic concept of altruism as put forward by Gary Becker in his economics of the family, establishing the basis for analysis of caring in New Home Economics (Chapter 3); the conceptualization of caring based on the concept of commitment by Amartya Sen and beyond (Chapter 4); the conceptualization of caring in a two-fold concept characterized by the centrality of the concept of a caring motivation as developed by Nancy Folbre, Susan Himmelweit, and others (Chapter 5). These concepts differ in the extent to which the "test case" of caring for dependents might be adequately incorporated. Although caring situations for dependents are not the focus of these concepts, their analysis provides insights into this extreme caring situation, thus giving us building blocks for the conceptualization of caring for dependents in economics. The questions which the above approaches leave unaddressed are treated in the further process of conceptualization.

Part III addresses the social organization of caring situations, their coordination, and institutionalization. The concept of a caring situation is developed to encompass the characteristics of caring activities in general and of caring for dependents in particular. In this framework, a caring situation is characterized by the effective performance of a caring activity and is analyzed by the use of three analytically separate but mutually contingent components: *motivation*, which is the benevolent, caring motivation needed for an effective caring situation to come about; *work*, which is the actual hands-on caring activity that must be performed to satisfy the care receiver's needs and which creates a direct caring relationship between care giver and care receiver; *resources,* which is the input necessary to support an effective caring activity. The task of the social organization of caring activities is understood as the job of effectively combining the three components in a way that is sensitive to the potential or actual asymmetries and dependencies in given caring situations. (Chapter 6)

The asymmetries and dependencies characteristic of caring situations for dependents have a decisive influence on the structure of the need for caring services as well as on their provision. And an integrated analysis of the caring situation must systematically take account of the asymmetries and dependencies involved in the provision of most caring activities, especially of caring for dependents. The different kinds of real and potential asymmetries and dependencies involved in caring situations (asymmetries in capabilities and existential dependency, asymmetries in resource control and material dependency, motivational barriers to exit and motivational dependency) are analyzed in greater detail. Special attention is given to the questions of whether, and the extent to which, structures underlying caring situations alleviate, aggravate, or even help generate asymmetries and dependencies. (Chapter 7)

In a last step, the analytical tools presented and developed in the study are integrated. Asymmetries and dependencies are identified as major coordinates for the social organization of caring situations for dependents. Sensitive points in the provision of caring situations for dependent care receivers are presented: the split between instrumental and communicative caring tasks, stratification within the groups of care givers and care receivers, tension between goals of self-realization and concern for others, and the ideological context. The study concludes that the long-term success of any economic domain (family, civil society, state, market) in which the social provision of caring activities takes place depends on the capacity of its institutional arrangements to take into account the actual or potential asymmetries involved, as well as any resulting potential or actual dependencies. The investigation closes by suggesting two directions for socio-economic policies: the further fostering of a diversified landscape of institutions providing caring situations, and further steps towards the achievement and materialization of care giver equity. (Chapter 8)

Chapter 2

THE ANALYTICAL FRAME OF REFERENCE

Basic characteristics of caring activities

To care is to consciously situate oneself in relation to the world, to the outer social and natural environment. The performance of a caring activity presupposes and involves the conscious establishment of relationships of the individual not only with other human beings but also with non-human entities, the environment and biosphere, plants, animals, objects, and the self. Caring activities are human activities that aim at the long-term maintenance, sustenance, and repair of these physical and social relationships which are indispensable for continuing human existence in a social context.[1]

The actual care giving activity is part of a larger process of caring. It involves some form of ongoing connection and continues through time. Caring is not necessarily confined to a relationship between (just) two individuals; it can also function socially and politically in a broader setting which, in turn, largely defines and shapes it. Caring has an intimately private side with regard to its products, as well as a decidedly public dimension. Caring activities, understood in this sense, are the very preconditions for human existence and thus also prerequisites for all other human activities.[2]

Focus on caring that affects persons

The following discussion concentrates on caring activities affecting persons and understands (existential) human needs as the quintessential object of caring.[3] Although the needs to which caring activities respond may be as diverse as feeding a hungry child, helping an elderly person dress, or taking a friend to the railway station, it is the response to an existential need which lies at the core of personal caring activities. Some of these needs are

---

[1] At the most general level, a caring activity can be viewed as "a species activity that includes everything that we do to maintain, continue, and repair our 'world' so that we can live in it as well as possible" (Fisher and Tronto 1990: 40).

[2] The effective provision of caring activities in this sense constitutes a fundamental pillar for the socially and ecologically sustainable performance of any economic system. (Jochimsen and Knobloch 1997)

[3] It will become apparent, however, that the main conceptual elements of caring affecting persons as discussed and analyzed in this study are transferable to caring affecting non-human entities.

biological, others psychological or emotional, some culturally defined and variable over time.

Caring activities as understood here refer to sustaining the care receiver, often by means of daily care. The degree of care that others have to provide depends on both culturally constructed and biologically conditioned differences. Caring activities affecting persons may be *other-regarding* or *self-regarding*. Three basic types of caring affecting persons may be analytically distinguished: *kinship or friendship care*, *caring for dependents*, and *self-care*. In concrete caring situations they may combine and co-exist with one another.

The needs of the other as starting point for action

Fundamental to other-regarding caring activities is the pre-eminent role of the needs of the person cared for over the caring person's own need in bringing the performance of a caring service about. Of defining importance for caring activities that affect others is "a perspective of taking the other's needs as the starting point for what must be done" (Tronto 1993: 105). It involves taking the concerns and needs of the other as the basis for action.[4] As such it implies reaching out to something other than the self, it presupposes some sort of connection or relatedness between the partners involved and is neither self-referring nor self-absorbing.[5]

The definition of what comprises adequate care in situations of need varies from culture to culture, from society to society, and among different groups within any society. It follows criteria of distinction, for example, according to affinity group, class, caste, and gender.[6] Conceptually, therefore, caring is both particular and specific, as well as universal. It is not universal with regard to any specific needs, but all humans have needs that others must help them meet; despite the fact that the meaning of caring varies for different societies and groups, care nonetheless concerns a universal aspect of human life.

The skills needed to meet the demands may involve intellectual or manual abilities. Some require formal training, others not. Whatever the needs, as long as the care giver can perform the necessary caring activity, there is a responsibility for him/her to do so, especially in the provision of caring for dependents.

---

[4] Although it is acknowledged that caring for others may also include the need of the care giver to care and, in this special case, may even be exclusively motivated by this need.

[5] On the different phases of the caring process – "caring about," "taking care of," "care giving," and "care receiving" – see Tronto 1993: 105-108.

[6] According to Tronto, such cultural constructs of "well cared-for" may even be characteristic of these groups. (Tronto 1993: 110)

Caring activities and caring services

Other-regarding activities of kinship or friendship care and of caring for dependents may be conceptualized in the existing terminology of economics as person-to-person caring *services*. In these cases the care giver performs an activity for the benefit of the care receiver, bringing about a change in the physical or mental condition of the care receiver (Hill 1977: 318), as in serving someone a cup of tea, changing an infant's diapers, or bathing a sick person. This, of course, implies that the nature of the caring activity in question must be such that it is capable of being performed by a person other than the care receiver him/herself.

Caring services, of course, do not necessarily have to be performed by a person other than the care receiver him/herself but may also be performed as *own account services* as in self-care, where care giver and care receiver are identical. Self-regarding caring activities may also be of *non-service quality* as in human activities that meet one's own biological needs such as sleeping, eating, or resting as well as studying, and leisure/pleasure activities. Own-account caring services and non-service caring activities play an important role with regard to the comprehensive understanding of the provision of caring activities in general and are to be included within the systematic conceptualization of caring activities in economics.[7]

Care for others and care for the self are strongly interlinked; any lack of attention to this circumstance may create conflict and moral dilemma. And while the focus of this study is on the conceptualization of caring as concern for *others* and the social providing of person-to-person caring services, self-care will continue to play an important role throughout the investigation.[8]

The defining importance of the care receiver's capabilities

Self-care, caring for kin or friends, and caring for dependents vary according to care receivers' ability to perform the caring activity by themselves. In the case of self-care activities, the care giver can perform the needed caring activity by her/himself and actually does so. In instances of

---

7 A significant part of activities of self-care, as care for others, also responds to existential needs. Receivers can perform the activities themselves and although they are as dependent on the performance of such existential activities as the receivers of caring services for dependents, they do not have to rely on others. The performance or non-performance of activities of self-care by economic agents, self-employed entrepreneurs, managers, workers, and care givers in the informal economy, no doubt, is of direct relevance to and linked with the productivity and efficiency of these input factors in the economic process. The provision of these replenishing activities of self-care for every individual must be assured, since other-care becomes necessary in cases where existential self-care is impossible or inadequate.

8 In economics, self-regarding caring activities – an often neglected aspect of the sufficient restoration over time of a working person's capacity to work productively within the team – are generally viewed as *pre- or post-economic* activities and not in need of specific analysis.

kinship care and friendship care, one may assume that the care receiver is generally capable of performing the caring service alone, but that someone else performs the service for the care receiver. In such cases of what may be termed *caring for equally or similarly capable actors* the performance of the caring service could, in principle, be assigned back to the care receiver.[9]

Self-care and kinship or friendship care stand in contrast to the third type which in many respects connotates the "classical" type of caring activities: caring for dependents.[10] Caring for dependents is the sustaining care provided for young children, the frail elderly, the sick, and the disabled who cannot survive or function within a given environment (possibly within any environment) without steadily caring personal assistance.[11] In these cases, self-care is impossible or insufficient. The neediness of the care receiver in these cases is extreme, not only in terms of the existentiality of the need concerned but also in terms of the extent to which the care receiver has to rely on another person for support.

This is especially apparent in child care, elderly care, and care for the sick and disabled. For here, the care receiver cannot perform the caring service as an own account service. Babies cannot, for example, prepare their own food; elderly persons might not be able to dress by themselves; and the sick need all-around assistance. The care receiver, in effect, has no choice but to rely on someone else for the performance of a vital service. In this case, if a person other than the care receiver does not provide the caring service, it is not provided at all; this may well have life-threatening or *existential* consequences.[12] The incapability for self-care can be taken as an

---

[9] In a sense, existentially needed caring for dependents and caring for equally capable persons constitute opposite ends of a dependency scale in the provision of caring activities for others. As analytical distinctions, they help clarify certain differences between typical caring situations and may help generate important points of reference which any care policies would have to take into account.

[10] Kittay uses the term "dependency work" (1999: 30) for this kind of caring services. Although I am not happy with the term, I will use it for the time being as it covers the same kind of activities I have described as "core or primary caring activities" in previous papers (Jochimsen 1998, 1998a) while evoking the extreme case unmistakenly in its phrasing. It is thus less easily confused with caring activities in general.

[11] Kittay refers to a caring relationship in which the care receiver is existentially dependent as "dependency relationship," and to the care giver performing dependency work as "dependency worker." (Kittay 1999: 30) Adopting Kittay's terminology, caring service for a dependent care receiver may be called a *dependency service*.

[12] In Kari Waerness' typology of three caring relationships (Waerness 1984), dependency work refers to "care-giving relationships where the people cared for are unable to provide services for themselves, in a given environment, because they have a disability, are ill, or too young and therefore dependent on a care-giver to provide services for them." The concept includes "spontaneous care relationships where care is offered on a reciprocal basis in emergency or crisis situations without incurring expectations of continuity" as far as cases of temporary illness or disability are concerned. Whereas the third type of caring relationships which

additional and aggravating indicator of the care receiver's situation of need. It may serve as an indicator of the care receiver's vulnerability and of the extent to which the care giver has to take the care receiver's need as a starting point for action.

Differences

Caring activities as discussed in this study differ from domestic work and affection-based work, although there may be overlaps. Domestic work, such as housework, while often done in conjunction with caring for persons (cf. e.g. Gardiner 1997: 182-207), should not be considered identical with the latter since it also includes caring services performed for non-human entities as well as non-caring activities. Moreover, caring for persons is performed not only within the household but also outside, for example in nurseries and nursing homes. Also, caring activities are not identical with affection-based work since (as will be discussed below) caring work can be done without the affective dimension since it may be motivated by considerations other than affection.[13]

Caring activities, according to the definition presented in this chapter, also differ from the work of professionals such as doctors, teachers, and therapists, as described by Eva F. Kittay[14] – even it the other-directed character of their work bears certain similarities and if, by improving the health, welfare, or education of their clients, they are essential contributors to caring situations. Professional intervention usually lacks the continuity aspect characteristic of performing the caring service itself and presupposes the ongoing provision of general caring activities over a longer period in time. Caring activities address and comprehend the whole life process of the care receiver. They generally do not feature intervention at a specific point in time or for a certain period of time. By contrast, doctors intervene in cases of specific need for a functionally specific medical service and, after its performance, step away. The point of intervention is usually aimed at "a carefully targeted set of concerns, for which the professional is trained [and which is generally quite costly]. Once the intervention is complete, the professional's responsibility is over." (Kittay 1999: 40)

Waerness distinguishes, namely, "personal service relationships which involve an unequal relationship between carer and cared for and where the person cared for could, physically, provide the services for him- or herself, but social and cultural expectations, economic and political status or physical force enable the cared for to command someone else's labour," does not apply to dependency relationships as conceptualized above as it refers to caring among individuals that, in principle, are equally capable.

[13] Caring is also not identical with emotional labor (Hochschild 1983, Steinberg and Figart 1999) since "not all emotional labor is caring labor, but caring labor is a type of emotional labor" (Himmelweit 1999: 34).

[14] Cf. e.g. Kittay 1999: 38-40.

Caring for dependents as conceptual point of reference

In its endeavor to systematically conceptualize the main features of caring activities and their provision for the purpose of economic theory, this study will take the crucial and undisputed classic cases of caring for dependents as its starting point and conceptual point of reference.

By focusing on child care and care for the elderly, the sick, and the disabled, all cases in which the care receiver relies existentially on the care giver, we do not want to imply that self-care and kinship or friendship care are not interesting objects of analysis or that their provision in private and in society does not raise problems. But there are several aspects that make caring for dependents a suitable and interesting point of reference for the conceptualization of caring activities in economics and for making it a "test case," the acid test for adequate conceptualization of caring.

Caring for dependents as practical bottleneck

One set of aspects involves the practical and existential importance of caring for dependents with pronounced vulnerabilities. Early childhood, illness, disability, and frailty in old age are inescapable phases of the human condition. These "inevitable dependencies" define and form at least parts of the life history of each individual. Human dependency is not an exceptional circumstance but rather an intrinsic, inalienable element of the human condition, a fact of everyone's individual life. (Kittay 1999: Chapter 1) The existential dependency of a person on the help of others normally undergoes significant changes during a person's lifetime. Furthermore, it may range in intensity. Phases of dependency can be extensive, including the extended dependency of early childhood, or brief with temporarily incapacitating illness. Dependency may also change in an unforeseen manner throughout one's lifetime. While some non-life-threatening illnesses can render the individual dependent for a limited period of time, other relatively minor disabling conditions can leave individuals seriously and even permanently dependent. Dependency can be both alleviated and aggravated by cultural practices and prejudices.

Caring for dependents is the existential task whose implementation must be assured by any societal organization. In this sense, caring for dependents constitutes the very core of caring activities. And caring for dependents accounts for a vast proportion of human caring interactions. The rationale behind focusing on this aspect is that, once we understand the implications of the most crucial and obvious cases of dependency, we can then appreciate the full range of caring activities and human interaction. Regardless of how dependency in caring situations may vary as a function of prevailing social understanding and technological constraints, the vulnerability of dependents creates a set of conditions under which attention must inevitably be given the needs of others. At some point in life, *every* human being needs outside help to meet her/his basic needs and, at some point in life, *every* human being might be called on to care for a dependent individual. For these reasons, this study uses caring for dependents, the classic caring situation, as the conceptual point of reference for theorizing care in economics.

Caring for dependents as theoretical bottleneck

In addition to the practical implications as discussed above, caring for dependents involves certain conceptual tasks deriving from the defining characteristics of caring. Specific to the situation of the dependent care receiver is the inability to perform the caring services needed as own-account services. Self-care is – by definition – impossible here or rather limited. The care receiver's autonomy is permanently or temporarily impaired or entirely lacking.

The limited or absent autonomy of the care receiver manifests itself in several directions. Autonomy may be limited with regard to the care receiver's inability to perform the caring service needed. But it may also reveal itself in additional respects. A frail elderly person, for example, who relies on a care giver, might mentally be well capable of precisely voicing and identifying the specific caring services required. In other cases, the limited autonomy of the care receiver might reveal itself as the inability to identify, specify, or express the precise caring service needed. This may be due to the age or state of mental and physical health of the care receiver. Young children, the severely ill, mentally confused or handicapped elderly, and disabled persons are hardly in a position to name and specify the kind of caring services needed from the care giver. In these cases a person other than the care receiver must identify the dependents' needs and determine how to satisfy them. The dependent care receiver's autonomy may also be limited or lacking with regard to the control of his/her own resources and, therefore, may be incapable of demanding the relevant caring services on the market. As a result, caring for dependents is typically characterized not only by the care receiver's incapability for self-care, but also by the outside identification of needs, the outside determination of preferences, and the outside control of resources.[15]

Accordingly, the dependent care receiver does not feature the characteristic so very central to the concept of the economic individual in economics, namely, autonomy. It is, after all, one of the core assumptions of the concept of the economic individual that she/he be autonomous in making decisions and choices based on her/his own preferences, not on someone

[15] This splitting of functions will be discussed in greater detail in Chapter 8.

else's – with limits imposed only as regards the information available. (e.g. Kirchgässner 2000: 16)

The limited or entirely absent autonomy of dependent care receivers, furthermore, has an impact on their capacity for providing returns to the care giver in terms of counter-actions in a general sense for the caring services performed on their behalf. In severe classic caring situations it is very likely that only a very limited or perhaps even *no* return might be derived from the care receiver.

Central conceptual assumptions

The decisive influence of the care receiver's situation on the performance of the caring activity is especially apparent in classic caring situations where the care receiver is incapable of performing the needed caring activity her/himself. This determinative influence, which dictates the kind of caring service to be performed by the care giver, calls for a shift in the perspective of analysis from the person performing the activity to the person affected by it.

These characteristics of the care receiver's vulnerable starting position have implications for the conceptual assumptions that can be sensibly made about provision of care for dependents. (Jochimsen 2003, 2003a) It is the working hypothesis of this investigation that, taken together, the main characteristics of caring for dependents make up a situation of providing that cannot be reduced to the idealtype exchange situation. The above-mentioned change in perspective requires a different, original, and specific set of conceptual assumptions that extend beyond that of independent, autonomous economic agents in full command of their physical and mental capabilities, free to chose their entry into or exit from (market) exchange situations; the assumptions take account of and are sensitive to the specific characteristics of caring situations for dependents. If account is to be taken of caring situations found in child care and care of the sick, elderly, and disabled, the systematic conceptualization and analysis of caring situations must presuppose a set of four basic conceptual assumptions:

(1) The assumption of relatedness

The analysis of caring situations assumes the relatedness of the specific (economic) individuals involved. Without the general assumption of relatedness between the two participating persons, the caring service would not be provided. For the dependent care receiver to be helped, another person must be nearby and take the dependent's needs as starting point for action. This other person must relate to the dependent's situation of need to be able to care. Furthermore, the intentions of the care giver must be so disposed as to help the care receiver.

The conceptualization of the individual as a person-in-relation makes it possible, as Julie Nelson suggests, that instead of a sharp differentiation between autonomous adults and dependent nonperson children, one can "envision a continuum of separation and connection" (Nelson 1996: 69) and between autonomy and dependency varying with age and the capacity for responsibility.

The decisive role played by the need of the *other* in constituting the starting point for any caring activity and determining the kind of caring activity to be performed, moreover, represents a shift in the perspective of analysis. For here, both partners involved are of interest to the analysis: the care giver and the care receiver alike, not just the person performing the activity but also the person affected by it.

As shall be shown in more detail in Part II, the assumption of relatedness is more specifically reflected in the assumptions about the care giver's motivations. These are generally taken to be benevolent rather than indifferent, and in any case they extend beyond purely self-interested or extrinsic motives.

(2) The assumption of asymmetries

As a consequence of the care receiver's limited autonomy, the analysis of caring situations further assumes that caring situations encompass qualitatively and quantitatively asymmetric relationships with respect to the differences in the starting positions of the partners involved.[16]

The asymmetries may be of various types. They may reflect the respective capacity of care giver and care receiver to perform the caring service (*asymmetry in capabilities*), they may also reflect their respective power to control the resources needed (*asymmetry in resource control*), they may reflect the motivational background of the persons involved in a caring situation (*asymmetry in motivation*), or the care receiver's inability to provide any or equivalent returns. These asymmetries may be conceptualized as unequal existential, material, and motivational options for entry into and exit from a caring situation.

The concept of asymmetry expresses these differences in quantity and quality in explicit terms on each side of the relationship. It allows for the identification and analysis of differences found in a dependency situation, thereby opening up the possibility of integrating them both in the conceptualization of caring activities as well as in the analysis of caring situations. This is of particular significance for conceptualizing caring

---

[16] Cf. also Biesecker 1996: 11-13.

situations for dependents. But it is also important for conceptualizing caring situations in general since the asymmetries mentioned are positioned on a graduated scale and may also be present in caring situations of the non-dependency type. From the perspective of asymmetric dependency relations, the symmetric relationship, as the special case of a caring situation where two equally capable partners meet, occupies a place at one end of the asymmetry scale.[17]

(3) The assumption of dependencies

The analysis of caring situations must also rely on the general assumption of the possible dependencies of the participating individuals, as is obvious in the provision of care for dependents, where the limited autonomy of the care receiver, together with asymmetries it might entail, accounts for the dependencies involved.

In this study, "dependency" will be understood as limited options of entry into and exit from caring situations, analogous to economics' common understanding of its opposite, "independence." The concept of independence in economics is closely connected to that of freedom of choice. The independent economic agent is an agent who is free to enter or exit an (exchange) situation. By contrast, dependency is to be understood as a force compelling entry and as a barrier blocking exit.[18] As shall be discussed in more detail below, asymmetries in caring situations may lead to *existential dependency*, *material dependency*, and *motivational dependency*, and under certain conditions to their exploitable forms.[19] In caring situations, possible dependencies of the persons involved more specifically include their limited control over the extent and kind of the caring service to be provided.

The respective asymmetries and dependencies in a caring or a dependency situation are not only manifested by the care receiver but may involve the care giver as well. The specific situations of care receiver and

---

[17] The concept of asymmetry, by allowing for graduated asymmetry, also includes the symmetric case, whereas the concept of symmetry, as there is no gradation in symmetry, is unable to encompass asymmetric relations.

[18] Dependency, therefore, also reflects the – not necessarily voluntary – relatedness of the individuals involved. In Western societies, dependency is a highly ideological term. In a world ruled by assumptions and values of personal autonomy and individual independence, the term has no easy standing. Yet, dependency has not always been negatively connotated. The term has undergone significant changes since the last century and "good dependency" has almost disappeared. (Fraser and Gordon 1997) Research on issues of care, however, reasserts the power of the concept of dependency to describe essential relations among human beings which exist alongside moments of autonomy. (e.g. Kittay 1999, Kittay and Feder 2003, Sevenhuijsen 1998: Chapters 1 and 2).

[19] On the changes in the connotation of the term "dependency" in the past centuries and the more abstract meanings of the term see Fraser and Gordon 1997.

care giver must be taken into account to understand the complex structures behind the provision of caring services.

The asymmetries and dependencies involved in caring situations may vary in degrees. They may be especially striking in the provision of caring for dependents and may be virtually absent in caring for kin or caring among equals. Yet, using caring for dependents as an idealtype understanding of an extreme and crucial caring situation allows us to concentrate on the asymmetries involved in the provision of caring services.

As shall be discussed in more detail in Part III (Chapters 7 and 8), the degrees of both the asymmetry involved and the dependency are shaped by i) the assumed capabilities of the care receiver with regard to self-care, ii) the critical nature of the needs to be cared for, iii) the institutional organization of access to and control over the resources needed to sustain a caring relationship, and iv) the ideological context in which the caring activity is provided.

(4) The assumption of inherent power structures

While the concept of independence knows issues of power and control only in the sense of their negation, the concept of dependency, at a very general level, is intrinsically associated with questions of power and control over the will formation and decision making potential of the participants in caring situations. The analysis of caring situations, therefore, assumes a power structure within the caring situation conceptualized as an unequal power outfit for the persons involved. It assumes that caring situations for dependents are inherently put together, shaped, and influenced by the power structures underlying them. Different kinds of power come into play. Power may be the physical capability and skill to perform a caring service. There is power at work in the control over and access to the resources needed for caring[20] as well as social and moral power in terms of who feels the responsibility to actually perform the caring work. The actual institutional manifestations of power, however, are as much the result of the asymmetric relations in the caring situation itself as that of the broader sociological, socio-psychological context, behaviors, attitudes, ethical norms, personal deviations, and role expectations in which the caring situation is embedded. These may be enhanced by societal structures. (Radin 1997: 154-163; Himmelweit 1997; Folbre 1994: Part I)

The conceptual differences between caring situations and economic exchange situations, and the step beyond assumptions of autonomy, symmetry, independence, and the absence of power open up possibilities and options for the analysis of caring situations beyond their interpretation

[20] E.g. in the public system of redistribution.

as exchange situations.[21] Within such an analytical framework, the graduated range of existential, material, and motivational asymmetries which characterize most caring situations, the resulting issues of the power structures among the persons involved, and their existential, material dependency and social-psychological dependency can be studied and discussed. With the above set of basic conceptual assumptions in mind, conceptual approaches already in use to explain caring in economics will be analyzed in Part II, and the social organization of effective caring situations will be studied in Part III.

---

[21] In economics, social interactions, i.e. actions which involve more than one individual, are commonly interpreted as exchange phenomena. (Kirchgässner 2000: 8)

II

CONCEPTUAL APPROACHES TO CARING IN ECONOMICS

Part II takes a closer look at approaches in economics which either explicitly aim at conceptualizing caring or are of relevance to the present discussion because they theorize altruism and commitment or otherwise touch upon the sensitive questions at hand. The main features of each approach will be outlined and its ability to allow for the inclusion of dependency situations explored.

The aim of the analysis is to examine the extent to which the concepts presented can incorporate caring services for dependents (the dependency situation). The result will be a collection of differently sized and differently important pieces of a puzzle examined and identified as such.

Rather than proceeding in chronological order, the search will move from the most familiar to the most open or unknown. The analysis will show the way and extent to which the basic characteristics of caring situations discussed in the previous chapters are reflected and have found entry into the conceptualization of caring in economics and shaped conceptual solutions. The proposed solutions presented in the following not only reflect the ongoing analytical task of integrating caring situations and economic theory; they also reflect the fact that caring for dependents constitutes a bottleneck not only in the provisioning of caring in general practice but also as regards the conceptualization of caring activities in economic theory. Conceptual approaches to caring in economics find themselves in a curious and interesting field of tension characterized on the one hand by the attempt to understand the provision of caring within the traditional analytical framework of economic science and on the other hand by the recognition of the need to develop new and additional analytical tools for an adequate conceptualization of caring.

Chapter 3

CARING AS THE RESULT OF PREFERENTIAL CHOICES

The conceptualization of caring in the utility-based concept of altruism

A familiar conceptual approach to caring in economics is to see it as behavior that enhances the utility of both care receiver and care giver and to model the satisfaction derived from enhancing the utility of another person within a preference-based, choice-oriented, and utility-maximizing concept of altruism. In a neoclassical framework, the common notion of altruism is modeled in terms of positively *inter*dependent utilities: applied to the provision of caring, this would mean that the utility functions of the care giver and the care receiver are assumed to be analytically inseparable. Since the utility of the care receiver is assumed to figure as one argument in the utility function of the care giver, enhancing the care receiver's utility by the performance of a caring service simultaneously amounts to enhancing the care giver's utility as well. Consequently, the care giver is regarded as an altruist willing to reduce his/her own consumption in order to increase the consumption of the care receiver (Becker 1976: 284) as long as doing so increases the care giver's own utility.[1] Caring is understood within the economic framework of utility considerations as preference-based choice behavior aiming at utility maximization. The performance of caring activities is understood as resulting from circumstances marked by scarcity and choice and explained by "the combined assumptions of maximizing behavior, market equilibrium,[2] and stable preferences" (Becker 1976: 5) characterizing the "economic approach." Decisions about caring are reached by weighing the advantages and disadvantages and the benefits and costs of alternative actions with the respective weighting determined by the preferences of the individual: caring is the result of a preferential choice.

Such an approach may be found most explicitly in New Home Economics (e.g. Becker 1976, 1981, 1996; Gustafsson 1993, 1994) which

---

[1] Interdependent utilities are not the only way to conceptualize altruism which also is defined as "the principle or practice of unselfish concern for or devotion to the welfare of others (opposed to egoism)" (Webster's Dictionary 1996). For other concepts see e.g. Komter 1996: 11 and Part III of her book.

[2] The assumption of market equilibrium implies that no one could do any better, otherwise they would.

studies and interprets caring behavior – like other kinds of human behavior – through the lens of utility-maximizing, consistent, forward-looking behavior.[3] Without being explicitly concerned with the conceptualization of caring services or extensively discussing the specific characteristics of caring and their impact on economic theorizing, New Home Economics opened the way to application of the neoclassical economic approach to caring behavior, thereby – if not necessarily by intention – having an impact on subsequent discussions on caring. Becker's model of the family has had "an enormous influence on modeling and information gathering the world over" (Nussbaum 2001: 63). The aim of discussing it here is to investigate the extent to which its approach to altruism, concerned with the sharing of resources such as income, wealth, and consumption goods, might be applicable to the subject of caring services. The intuition is that, in investigating this approach to determine if it might be applicable to the subject of caring services and – more specifically – to dependency services, several problems involved in the conceptualization of caring activities will be uncovered which go beyond the specific approach in question but offer a guide for further questioning.

In Becker's writings, two implicit concepts of caring may be detected, although the author himself neither defines nor develops them as such. The first might be called *caring between equally capable adults*, the second *caring for children*.

The first concept is chiefly developed in Becker's theory of marriage (Becker 1976: 205-250), but also carried further in his writings on social interaction and altruism (Becker 1976: 253-294, 1996: 139-161). Caring itself is measured through utility and conceptualized by interdependent utility functions. The two partners are each assumed to have a utility function in which the consumption of one partner influences the utility of the other. The assumption is that the commodity consumption of the care receiver matters in the utility function of the care giver (Becker 1976: 234): a reduction in the care receiver's consumption thus also lowers the care giver's utility. The respective partners are assumed to maximize their utility functions by the provision of caring services. The care receiver's income exceeds his/her own consumption if he/she also benefits from the care giver's consumption. The provision of a caring service for the care receiver, accordingly, is the result of a (voluntary) utility calculation of the care giver.

---

3 According to Becker, this approach is "a comprehensive one that is applicable to all human behavior, be it behavior involving money prices or imputed shadow prices, repeated or infrequent decisions, large or minor decisions, emotional or mechanical ends, rich or poor persons, men or women, adults or children [...], patients or therapists [...]" (Becker 1976: 8). In his book *The Economic Approach to Human Behavior* (1976), Becker himself interprets marriage, divorce, fertility, and relations among family members through the lens of utility-maximizing, forward-looking behavior.

In the case of a successful caring relationship between adults (spouses in Becker), caring is assumed to be *mutual*; both persons are care givers as well as care receivers. The extent to which the utility of the care receiver matters to the care giver, furthermore, is assumed to indicate the extent of caring, with "full" caring being the case if the care giver cared as much about the care receiver as about him/herself, i.e. if the care receiver's consumption mattered as much as the care giver's own consumption.

The conceptualization of caring between equally capable adults within the preference based model of economic altruism encompasses some of the constitutive features of caring mentioned above from a utility perspective, namely, the assumption that the care receiver's utility matters to the care giver, and that to improve the care receiver's situation there is a transfer of resources from the care giver to the care receiver. This concept of caring implies *sharing* conceptualized as the voluntary transfer of resources from one mate to the other, as well as the voluntary transfer of commodities between mates. Caring, conceptualized as receiving utility from someone else's consumption, induces people to transfer resources to this person (as well as commodities produced by the household) since "a person who is much better off than a spouse she loves helps him out with money and in other ways. These contributions reduce the inequality of their resources." (Becker 1996: 234) The sharing is assumed to be equal when the caring is full and mutual.[4] (Becker 1976: 235)

The assumption that mutual full caring involves equal sharing reveals that caring between two adults is conceptualized as being *symmetric* – at least as far as the autonomy of the persons involved is concerned: both partners are care givers as well as care receivers. This presupposes that each of the two is able to be a care giver – in Becker's framework, to share, i.e. to transfer resources. The caring abilities (of spouses) must be (at least roughly) equal as far as their endowment with resources and commodities is concerned.[5] The underlying assumption of market equilibrium also suggests that within this model of interdependent utility functions care givers and care receivers have equal options and choices of voluntary entry and exit from the caring relationship.[6] In the economic concept of altruism the basic assumptions of economic behavior in the market (symmetry, voluntary behavior, choice etc.) can therefore be maintained and "altruism is easily

---

4 Becker here seems to imply the tendency toward an equalization of the resources of the two partners in a relationship of caring between adults.

5 Note an important difference from Becker's theory of the family where the altruistic head of the household is the person controlling the resources and distributing them among the members of the household.

6 Criticisms of Becker's altruist model for its neglect of the issue of power, and in this sense the absence of symmetry, have been raised, among others, by Pollak 1985; McCrate 1987; Folbre 1988; England 1993; Strassmann 1993a, 1993b; Nelson 1996.

incorporated into standard models by the mechanism of interdependent utility functions" (Nelson 1996: 71).

Such a concept of caring which casts caring situations as exchange situations has a type of caring in mind that differs from dependency work. The kind of caring Becker is referring to when conceptualizing caring among equally capable adults is obviously less connected with the existential needs of personal survival and appears more voluntary and within the realm of choice. Not caring, of course, may prove to be less beneficial to the marriage as well as its production of family commodities and income. It is unlikely, however, that anyone in such a caring relationship would be exposed to a threat to survival if this caring among equals were not performed – although not caring could well cause suffering and even separation.

The concept of psychic income

The utility argument with regard to altruism is based on the firm conviction that "a person makes contributions to add to his own utility – otherwise he would not part with any wealth" (Becker 1996: 232). In this sense altruism operates analogously to selfishness in an exchange situation. The notion that caring behavior seeks to maximize the care giver's utility goes along with the need to conceptualize a return from the care receiver's side. Thus, for the concept of interdependent utilities to work, it is assumed that the care giver receives something in return for behavior advanced toward the care receiver, which might figure as utility to the care giver. In the absence of pecuniary or other material rewards, the return is "psychic income" (Becker 1976: 175). If no pecuniary or material advances are to be expected, either because the care receiver is too young (as in the case of children) or material return is not of prominence in the informal private sphere, the performance of caring services is assumed to generate psychic income to the care giver.[7] (cf. also e.g. Becker 1996: 232)

Altruism thus understood always presupposes some sort of income to the altruist as a prerequisite. Without this kind of psychic income or without other kinds of utility being rendered to the care giver, the caring service would not be performed. It is important to keep this in mind as characteristic of the most common use of the concept of altruism in economics. Although the enhancement of the care receiver's utility is included and matters, it is always the care *giver's* utility which is maximized by the performance of a caring service. In that sense, it can be argued that within the concept of economic altruism the care giver's behavior is still self-interested since the care giver's utility function is still the one to be maximized and the pursuit

[7] This very circumstance, however, is characteristic but not defining for caring activities as psychic income may also arise from other and even from explicitly non-caring activities.

of the care giver's utility may thus be helped by altruistic action. This self-interest may be called *attached self-interest* to distinguish it from the commonly un-attached (or pure) self-interest assumed of individuals in markets. Still, it does not amount to *other*-interest – so important in caring.

A return on caring services, however, might also be assumed without reference to the concept of psychic income as reflected in the assumption that altruistic preferences are fostered by expectations of long-term reciprocity, for example, and the argument that altruistic preferences "may be somewhat endogenous, because if they remain entirely unappreciated they often dissipate over time" (Folbre and Weisskopf 1998: 175). According to Folbre and Weisskopf, expectations of reciprocity matter to the extent that their disappointment may induce care givers to change their altruistic preferences.[8] The authors argue that in the long run even parents and spouses or partners who provide loving care for their children or partners out of genuine affection "after a certain point [...] expect their care to be reciprocated to some extent. If this expectation is completely disappointed their preferences may change" (Folbre and Weisskopf 1998: 175). The implications of these assumptions about a return on caring, especially for dependency situations, will be further discussed below.

Parental care for children

The central importance of the assumption of symmetric autonomy when modeling caring behavior as deriving from interdependent utility functions of care giver and care receiver reveals its full significance in Becker's model of parents' caring behavior toward their children. Since children – especially infants – are to be considered as having only limited autonomy, Becker puts forward a different concept of caring. The care receiver, the child, is not conceptualized as an equal, autonomous partner with an independent utility function whose consumption is integrated into the utility function of the care giver. Rather, children are conceptualized as "passive nonpersons" (Nelson 1996: 68), as durable consumption or production goods and, as such, figure in their parents' utility functions as a source of psychic income or satisfaction. The care receiver is conceptualized as being "produced" by the parents' caring services as a durable family consumption or production commodity.[9] Child care in this framework is to be understood as the parents'

---

8 In this assumption Folbre and Weisskopf differ from Becker who assumes that preferences are stable over time. (Becker 1976: 5)

9 Although Becker's basic framework considers children as consumption goods (Becker 1976: 176), they are considered a production good if they provide monetary income – since "neither the outlays on children nor the income yielded by them are fixed but vary in amount with the child's age, making children a durable consumption and production good" (Becker 1976: 172). The net cost of children according to Becker "equals the present values of expected outlays plus the imputed value of the parents' services, minus the present value of the expected money

services toward a consumer durable (as one factor in the decision to raise children or not), from whose consumption (psychic) income in the form of (psychic) utility or satisfaction is expected. But modeling caring toward children in such a way inhibits the danger that selfish parents might "produce" their children merely to their own personal advantage and disregard the utility of the children (Becker 1996: 127-128)[10] since the care receiver's utility function is no longer part of the care giver's. As a counterbalance, Becker assumes "benevolence toward children (and occasionally others)" (Becker 1976: 282). His doing so marks an exception since the preference-based approach to human behavior generally does not include an assumption about specific motivations. Although it allows for a much richer set of values and preferences motivating human behavior beyond pure selfishness or mere material gain, it simultaneously assumes that the specific kind of motivation which drives any specific behavior does not matter, and that "individuals maximize welfare *as they conceive it,* whether they be selfish, altruistic, loyal, spiteful" (Becker 1996: 139; emphasis in the original).

However, the conceptualization of caring behavior would seem to require an exception in this approach – not only in terms of the assumption of interdependent utility functions but also as regards the assumption of a special motivation in this context. According to Becker, motivation behind caring within a family context matters characteristically and decisively. Relations among family members are conceptualized as "radically [different] from those among employees of firms and members of other organizations" (Becker 1996: 151). It is assumed that the preferences of a caring individual go beyond pure self-interest and critically depend on the care giver's altruism and feelings of duty and obligation toward the people cared for and that interactions among family members are "more likely to be motivated by affection, obligation, guilt, and a sense of duty than by self-interest narrowly interpreted" (Becker 1996: 151).

It is important to note here that the term altruism in the literature cited above appears to be used in two differing senses. On the one hand, it connotes a *motivation* behind caring. On the other, it is used in the meaning of a *specific relationship between two persons' utility functions*. Although

---

return plus the imputed value of the child's services. If net costs were positive, children would be, on balance, a consumer durable and it would be necessary to assume that psychic income or utility was received from them" (Becker 1976: 175). Why – one might add – would people in a framework of welfare calculation otherwise care for children? Note that elsewhere in Becker, children are also conceptualized as having their own utility functions as revealed, for example, by the "Rotten Kid Theorem." (Becker 1976: 270; Becker 1996: 151)

[10] Still, according to Becker, even selfish parents transfer resources to their children, try to shape their tastes, and do not treat them poorly since they hope for their children's help in old age. (Becker 1996: 127-128)

related, the two concepts are not identical, since the economic concept of altruism as positively interdependent utility functions is taken to reflect not only altruistic motivations and their variations[11] but also motivations such as duty, obligation, affection, etc. If these different motivations are all translated into the altruistic utility calculus, however, no conceptual room is left to distinguish between motivations based on utility considerations and moral or other intrinsic motivations that are not based on a utility calculus. The different quality of moral or other intrinsic motivations and their importance with respect to the provision of caring services is then lost. In this study, altruism will be used in the sense of interdependent utilities as described above and be understood as the only motivation covered by this concept.

The concept of "household or family commodities"

A concept central to Becker's utility-based approach to caring in the non-market sphere is the concept of household or family commodities.[12] *Household or family commodities* in Becker's framework are goods and services produced by each household partly with market goods and services and partly with different household members' own time. Household-produced commodities include the quality of meals, the quality and quantity of children, prestige, recreation, companionship, love and other emotional attachments, and health status.[13] These commodities are assumed to be more efficiently produced in households than in the market because individual behavior is assumed to be altruistic (attachedly self-interested) in the household and self-interested (unattachedly self-interested) in the market.

Caring services between equally capable adults in Becker's approach are conceptualized as a household or family commodity and part of the production of family commodities that are jointly consumed. In this framework, adults care for adults on order to maximize their own utility through the consumption of household-produced commodities, and they do

[11] For special forms of altruism as conceptualized within the rational choice framework of experimental economists see Chapter 5.

[12] While commonly labeled as "household" or "family," the relationships modeled, however, are in practice models of marital couples. Children are either invisible in the formal models (e.g. Chiappori 1988), or treated as goods (e.g. Manser and Brown 1980). For a critique of the general invisibility of children in economic modeling see Levison 2000.

[13] Household commodities cover a broad range of human activities and aims and cannot be identified with consumption or output as usually measured. Becker assumes, however, that all commodities can be combined into a single aggregate making the maximization of utility for each person equivalent to maximizing the amount of the aggregate received. (Becker 1976: 207-208)

so by their own choice. (Becker 1976: 232)[14] The more people in a household who care, the greater the amount of family commodities. (Becker 1976: 236) According to Becker, the same holds true with regard to child care. Taking the quality of children as an indicator for the care they received, caring activities are also conceptualized as a family commodity since children themselves, and their quantity and quality, are conceptualized as a commodity to be consumed exclusively by the members of the household. (Becker 1976: 207)

The central prerequisites for the production of household or family commodities are the physical and/or social closeness of the producers since it is assumed that the care giver could best transfer commodities to the care receiver if they both lived in the same household. Moreover, resources are more cheaply transferred within households and household commodities are only transferable within and not between households. According to Becker, caring thus provides an incentive for living together at the same time as it is encouraged by living together.[15] The conceptual insistence on close interaction stresses the personal relationship, the person-to-person situation necessary for the performance of caring services. Caring services conceptualized as family commodities are considered neither "marketable nor transferable among households, although they may be transferable among members of the same household" (Becker 1976: 207). The most important assumption concerning family commodities is that the third-party criterion (Reid 1934: 11) does not apply.[16] Caring services so conceptualized are consumed exclusively by the members of the same household and are thus conceptualized as intimately private goods.[17]

---

[14] Becker examines the effect of love and caring between mates on the nature of equilibrium in the marriage market. Becker's simplified model of marriage relies on two basic assumptions: first, that "each person tries to find a mate who maximizes his or her well-being" (Becker 1976: 232) and that this well-being may be measured by the consumption of household-produced commodities; and second, that "the 'marriage market' is assumed to be in equilibrium, in the sense that no person could change mates and become better off" (Becker 1976: 232).

[15] This conceptualization is quite common although most of the time it is attributed to the emotional motivation involved rather than the utility increase to be expected. (e.g. Folbre 1995)

[16] According to the third-party criterion, someone who is not a member of the household but coming from outside (i.e. the market) could produce these services to the same effect. This manner of distinguishing productive from non-productive activities has been criticized by Cynthia Wood for its "implicit market standard for defining nonmarket economic activity" (Wood 1997: 47).

[17] This conception is fostered and reinforced by stressing the importance of private emotional attachments for the performance of caring activities. Becker understands love as affectionate concern for the well-being of another, and states that "loving someone usually involves caring about what happens to him or her" (Becker 1976: 233-234).

The scope of the concept

In assessing the scope of conceptualizing caring within the above-sketched economic framework of altruism, three main areas shall be discussed: the impossibility of taking adequate account of and depicting properly dependency situations within interdependent utility functions, the insensitivity of the preference approach towards moral and other intrinsic motivations, and the confinement of the concept to the informally private sphere of the economy.

The inability to take adequate account of dependency situations

The conceptualization of caring within the utility-based framework of economic altruism produces a concept that might work for a caring situation between equally capable adults. It assumes the interdependence of the care giver's and the care receiver's utility function, conceptualizing the care receiver as an autonomous individual with a utility function of his/her own. Caring is conceptualized as (1) person-to-person interaction characterized by (2) interdependent utility functions (economic altruism) of care giver and care receiver. Caring is understood as (3) the result of a utility calculation, a cost-benefit analysis that takes into account the commodity consumption of both partners; the extent of caring is understood as the degree to which someone else's consumption matters in a person's utility function. Caring is further assumed (4) to involve sharing, that is, the voluntary transfer of resources and household commodities from care giver to care receiver. Caring is conceptualized as (5) voluntary and apparently (6) not intrinsic to the survival of any of the persons since it is assumed that care giver and care receiver can leave the situation at any given time.

Through the economic concept of altruism, the utility of the person cared for can conceptually be brought into the discussion. Asymmetry can thus be addressed, although only to a certain extent since there is the conceptual tendency to equalize asymmetric situations via the assumptions made, as has been shown with regard to caring between adults. This tendency requires that asymmetry and dependency be overlooked. Also, one of the basic assumptions of the utility concept is a return for services provided, which could figure as utility to the care giver. The care receiver or the behavior towards her/him must accordingly always produce something in return – if not pecuniary then psychic income. Extending the concept of psychic income to be all-inclusive – at the expense of analytical clarity – would, however, render it useless.

It has been argued by many economists that to rely on individuals' (material) self-interest is the safest way to secure desired behavior (Kirchgässner 1996, 1997) and that to rely on anything else would be rather risky. From the dependency perspective, however, the argument seems to work the other way around. From the point of view of the dependent care receiver it seems to be rather risky to have to rely on the (occasional) self-interest of the care giver, especially on his/her material self-interest.

Modeling caring with the tools of a theoretical approach based on assumptions of symmetry and autonomy has two important implications. In both cases, potentially underlying asymmetries and dependencies are absent from the theoretical picture and are neither discussed nor analyzed – a circumstance which is especially unsatisfying with regard to the conceptualization of caring situations for dependents.

In the conceptualization of caring between equally capable adults the partners involved are assumed to be autonomous agents equally capable of sharing and having equal options for entry to and exit from the caring situation. The concept thus suggests and emphasizes the similarity of the caring situation to (symmetric) exchange situations and ignores potentially underlying asymmetries and dependencies.

Assumptions of symmetry, although disputed,[18] would not appear to be entirely unfeasible (at least for analytical purposes) when constructing a model for caring relationships between adults. But this can hardly be true for dependency situations such as child care. When the preference-based approach is applied to caring for persons with limited autonomy such as children, the assumption of interdependent utility functions is replaced by a completely different construction, namely the assumption that the care receiver figures as a durable consumption or production good among commodities which render utility to the care giver. Unlike caring among equally capable adults, caring for children (1) cannot be conceptualized as a relationship between two persons with interdependent utility functions; rather (2) the care receiver in this framework must be conceived as a consumer durable that is one item in the utility function of the care giver. Caring for children appears as (3) the result of a utility calculation involving the cost and benefits of child care assuming a return to the parents in form of psychic income. While the assumption of choice can be maintained since caring for children is conceptualized as (4) voluntary from the parents' point of view, since they care for their children by choice, the assumption of purely self-interested behavior must be abandoned since caring for children is assumed to be (5) characterized by the prevalence of benevolence towards children. The product of child care, the quality (and quantity) of children, is also conceptualized as a household or family commodity and therefore as an exclusively private good.

The conceptually stated difference between the parent-child relationship as a person-to-consumer-durable relationship and the person-to-person

[18] Cf. Fn. 6 of this chapter.

relationship between two autonomous persons has not been recognized by Becker. In his framework there is no explanation of why interdependent utility functions apparently do not apply in the modeling of child care – or why an adult partner in a partnership is not conceptualized as a consumer durable or the earning spouse as a producer durable. After all, adults also receive psychic income from one another. Yet children are conceptualized as family commodities, and "produced" – mates are not.

The conceptionalization of caring for children in the described manner reveals the difficulty of the utility approach to fully capture aspects of asymmetric situations involving dependents by means of analytical tools that presuppose symmetry and autonomous agents.

A child care situation is a typical dependency situation. Its most prominent feature is the inherent asymmetry of the capabilities of the persons involved: the care receiver's limited autonomy and her/his existential dependency on the care giver to perform the caring service. A child care situation is neither symmetric with regard to the care giver's and care receiver's capabilities to perform the caring service, nor with regard to options for voluntary entry or exit. Also, there can be no *mutual* sharing (at least not as long as the child is very young) in the sense of the mutual sharing between adults conceptualized above since there can be no transfer of resources from child to parent. This asymmetry makes crucial the assumption that psychic income or utility was received from the child cared for since net costs in most cases are positive.

The inherent asymmetry and dependency of the child care situation, which is characterized by the utter dependency of the child, results in the hesitation to see the child as an equal autonomous partner in the caring relationship. Within a neoclassical theoretical framework that only allows for the conceptualization of people as autonomous agents, non-autonomous children must be conceptualized as nonpersons. The conceptualization of a child care receiver as a nonperson, as a family commodity, is the conceptual consequence of the theoretical tools used in Becker's economic approach to human behavior.

The vulnerable status of dependent care receivers could not be more apparent than in their losing their status as persons. At the same time, the power which the care giver holds over the care receiver, due to the care giver's capability to perform the caring service, could not be more explicitly stated than by conceptualizing the care giver as the "producer" of the care receiver.

The assumption of benevolence with regard to child care might also be explained as reflecting the asymmetry and dependency involved in a dependency situation. The motivation of the care giver is of importance in the conceptualization of a dependency relationship even within a concept which usually makes no use of assumptions of special motives. It is the absence of symmetry which calls for this assumption, because children cannot survive without the presence of benevolence. It is precisely because the parent-child relationship is marked by asymmetry in various respects that the assumption of benevolence on the parents' side is crucial – while with regard to caring among equally capable adults no special benevolent motivation is assumed.[19] (Becker 1976: 207-214) Children in their dependent position have no way of counteracting selfish treatment by care givers and can easily be taken advantage of.

Even if one followed Becker's conceptualization, the question remains whether the model of child care may be taken as a more general model of a dependency situation. In some crucial aspects it would seem to be inadequate in capturing the dependency situation. Can Becker's concept of child care be taken to encompass other kinds of dependency situations? More specifically, is Becker's conceptual framework of child care transferable to caring for dependent adults as care for the sick, the elderly, and the disabled? In these caring relationships the dependent sick, elderly, or disabled adult might be just as incapable with regard to performance of the caring service as the child relative to the care giver. The dependent adult might have an equally limited choice for entering or leaving the caring relationship. The dependency relationship in this sense is similar to a child care relationship. Yet, these are situations in which two adults engage, although not on terms of equal capabilities and in many cases not on the same autonomy terms. Which of the two concepts would be used to analyze and conceptualize such caring situations? If it seems implausible to treat infants and children as rational autonomous agents how must very sick, severely disabled, and frail elderly adults be treated? Is the concept of dependents as consumption or production goods for their care givers also feasible for adult dependents? After all, many other dependents are adults and much closer to being autonomous agents than children, e.g. the elderly parent who needs help to dress but otherwise can fully take his/her own decisions, or the temporarily incapacitated victim of an accident or illness.

How would one have to model a relationship of adult-child to adult-aging parent in this framework? Would one assume interdependent utility functions in these cases? Or is one to regard the aging parent as a consumer durable in the adult-child's utility function? Can children "produce" their elderly parents just as parents in Becker's concept decide to "produce" children?[20]

---

[19] In a sense, therefore, the motivational background to caring remains vague.

[20] These children will presumably be able-bodied, healthy children as "children of many qualities are usually available, and the quality selected by any family is determined by tastes, income, and price" (Becker 1976: 175), and apparently less by genes, accidents, fate, inevitable dependencies, etc. Also, the concept of children as the parents' choice may involve the idea of

The conceptualization of family members "either as independent, autonomous individuals, or as passive nonpersons who can be subsumed into someone else's preferences or into the constraints" (Nelson 1996: 68-69) reflects a "distorted [because one-sided] conception of human identity" (Nelson 1996: 69). Paula England (1993) argues that the basis of such conceptions is a separative model of human nature emphasizing autonomy and independence.[21] No concept of a dependent (sick, disabled, frail elderly) adult person exists. Children as dependents are conceptualized as nonpersons, as consumption (or production) goods. The conceptualization of child care based on the assumption of nonpersons points to the difficulties which arise when attempting to integrate dependency work into the theoretical body of utility-based economic thinking.[22] The unresolved question here is the conceptionalization of dependent persons. The focus on fully capable autonomous agents and the absence of asymmetry and dependency in a concept that shapes social interaction leaves this approach void of a concept for a dependent person. As Nelson has noted, "if [economists] persist in characterizing people as people only insomuch as they can be seen as autonomous agents – requiring the world be fitted into [the economists'] norms of methodological individualism – [the economists'] modeling stops here." (Nelson 1996: 65) As a consequence, dependents have been "almost entirely omitted from mainstream economic (and political) theory" (Badgett and Folbre 1999: 315).

Insensitivity to the importance of moral and other intrinsic motivations – confinement to the utility argument

Within the economic concept of altruism, caring is conceptualized as preferential choice. Altruism motivates one to act if another's situation makes one feel personally worse off. The concern for others directly affects one's own welfare. It can be argued, therefore, that behavior based on

---

the perfect child and entail the danger of fostering arguments for genetic engineering or selective abortion.

[21] England calls the model "'separative' because it presumes that humans are autonomous, impervious to social influences, and lack sufficient emotional connection to each other to make empathy possible" (England 1993: 37) – at least as far as their behavior in "the economy" or "the market" is concerned. England also points out that an, "often more implicit, assumption in many neoclassical models is that individuals do *not* behave according to the separative model vis-à-vis their families. Thus, empathic emotional connections between individuals are emphasized in the family whereas they are denied in analyzing markets" (England 1993: 37). But according to England, these assumptions "exaggerate both the atomistic, separative nature of behavior in markets and the connective empathy and altruism within families" (England 1993: 37).

[22] The concept has been widely criticized, for example by Blau, Ferber and Winkler 1998; Bergmann 1995; Nelson 1998.

altruism, although involving the utility of another person, is still self-interested in an important sense since the pursuit of one's own utility may be helped by altruistic action. There is the tendency to assume returns for anything given, be it in the shape of "psychic income," be it deferred returns as in the case of long-term expectations of reciprocity. The idea of exchange, so central to economic reasoning, prevails even when considering and conceptualizing caring situations. This principal characteristic, featured by concepts of altruistic preferences within a rational choice framework, also extends to special forms of altruism as discussed in Chapter 5 since these are also modeled as interdependent utility functions where the utility of the agents not only depends on the agents' own material payoff but also on how much the other players get.

Not in all instances, however, is the assumption of caring services rendering utility to the care giver tenable, and not in all cases is caring the result of a preferential choice. The economic concept of altruism, by its very nature, is limited in scope to caring situations that result from preferential choices to maximize the utility of the care giver. This might describe those cases of caring where utility considerations are involved. But other possible considerations for caring are also feasible and must be at work since utility considerations alone cannot explain caring in severe cases of dependency. Because motives behind caring are not differentiated within the utility approach of altruism but are all translated into the utility calculus, the specifics of non-utility based motivations such as moral considerations and other intrinsic motivations remain invisible.

The utility argument thus has certain shortcomings in connection with the appropriate treatment of dependency situations. Since it relies on psychic income or other forms of utility returns, altruistic caring behavior may be risky and humiliating for the care receiver who has to produce the two. For cases of very severe dependency or cases outside familiar small communities, the concept of altruism may be insufficient (Nelson 1998) in so far as it appears to be risky for dependents to rely on someone else's altruistic preferences for the caring services they need to survive.[23] This may be one of the reasons why much of caring for dependents in human society is structured by moral considerations such as duty, obligation, and responsibility. What if a child loses utility over her/his lifetime? How – if only behaving altruistically – would parents treat children from whom in the worst-case scenario no long-term reciprocity of any kind may be expected because of severe disabilities or lifelong sickness? Although Becker deals with questions such as addiction, drugs, and similar societal questions, he evades issues of disability, sickness, and lifelong dependency. What twists

---

[23] On the insufficiency of altruism with respect to the conceptualization of caring situations for dependents see Chapter 5.

and turns would have to be assumed to retain the altruistic utility calculation in some of these cases? Yet even the bottleneck cases of caring for dependents – where the care receiver will not be able to transfer resources back to the care giver at any point in time or where not much psychic income can be derived – must be able to be treated within the scope of the theoretical concept. People by whom no long-term reciprocity may be expected and who do not render psychic income must also be cared for. The ability to incorporate such a scenario is the test for any theory of caring in economics.

The task remains of conceptualizing caring behavior as other-regarding behavior that is performed without expectation of return – not even in terms of long-term or intergenerational reciprocity. In other words, the task is to conceptualize situations of human interaction in economics as gifts, as sustained one-way transfers – without assuming even an implicit or deferred exchange pattern. Caring behavior is strongly other-regarding behavior and not all caring behavior asks for returns. In fact it has been argued that caring situations presuppose something irreducible to exchange. Caring services and especially dependency services may be performed as one-way transfers without anticipation of return – not even in terms of reciprocity. Especially with respect to situations of extreme dependency of the care receiver (the test case of this study) one must allow for the fact that the care receiver will not be able to return the dependency service given or any equivalent either at present or in future. But such dependents also have to be cared for and, indeed, are cared for by dependency workers.

The assumption that no return is given, apart from the benefit of the care receiver, touches on two different lines of further argument. The no-return assumption can be discussed on the basis of welfare and utility calculations. But it may also involve motivations that are *not* based on utility and welfare calculations. (see Chapter 5)

Confinement to the informal domestic sphere

The concept of economic altruism helps bring to light important constitutive features of caring: the fact that the welfare of the care receiver matters to the care giver, that something intimately personal is created, and that part of the change induced by a caring service is not transactable and marketable but very personal. By presupposing and at the same time requiring intimacy (i.e. physical and social closeness) for the production and consumption of caring as the salient constitutive feature, caring is conceptualized as intimately and exclusively private, non-transactable, and voluntary. The important role of the production of household commodities confines both the concept and the analysis of caring to the household, thus to the informally private sphere. This is not materially changed by extending the study of altruism to other locations of physical and social interaction and physical closeness such as the neighborhood and the workplace[24] and acknowledging that contributions of time or goods may also be made to unrelated persons or to organizations desiring to improve the general well-being of recipients and exhibiting charitable or philanthropic behavior. (Becker 1976: 273) However, as changing social structures and professional mobility increase the geographical distances separating family members, at least in industrialized countries, Becker's conditions for caring in the family and neighborhood are found less and less, putting the development and the spill-over effects of altruism to a severe test.[25]

No concept of a caring situation per se, i.e. before and independent of its institutional setting in the family, neighborhood, or workplace, is developed. The conceptualization of caring as an intimately private product confines the concept and its scope of analysis to the informal, unpaid realms of the economy. Yet, by their existence and proximity to social interaction there is a public side to caring activities (e.g. Folbre 1994: 254, Plantenga 1998, England and Folbre 1999, 1999a); caring activities contribute to the creation of human and social capital. (England and Folbre 1999a: 45) If caring needs are privately met, society as whole benefits. The products of caring services, the changes which caring services induce, can also be conceptualized as a public good, a merit good.[26]

Connected with these considerations is the question of whether it would be feasible to extend the individual level to the societal level. What would happen if all caring were provided within altruistic frameworks? Would society continue to exist or would it break down because a decisive number of dependents would not be cared for?

In a concept of child care, which conceptualizes children as household commodities, it is also difficult to explain and understand, why people other than parents would care for, "produce," children – especially if they were not living in their respective household. Why, from a utility perspective, would anyone else but those living in the household care for children (even for selfish reasons)? That parents are conceptualized as the "producers" of their children may be derived from the biological process of bringing children into existence. But would this concept be equally conclusive if the participants in this caring relationship were others, from outside the household?

---

[24] Because economic altruism requires physical and social interaction, rather than common genes as a socio-biological model would do, it also explains "the survival of some altruism toward unrelated neighbors or coworkers" (Becker 1976: 294).

[25] Not to speak of the possibility of Becker's concept of altruism with regard to the virtual society on the Internet, which operates without physical closeness.

[26] This approach has been taken by Health Economics for example. See e.g. Gäfgen 1990: 14; Herder-Dorneich 1980: 7-10; Andreas 1994: 174-178.

Summary

Becker's utility approach focuses on the production of household or family commodities and, although capable of including small neighborhood communities and the workplace, the concepts of caring are confined to the informal, private, unpaid domestic realm of the economy as no conceptual distinction is made between the non-transactable communicative and the transactable instrumental aspect of caring. The motivational background remains ultimately unclear, since moral and utility considerations are mixed and attached self-interest prevails.

The conceptionalization of caring within the economic concept of altruism as discussed in this chapter covers one layer of the multi-layered caring situation and helps analyze some caring situations. To study the caring situation more comprehensively, however, one has to look at other concepts as well. As shall be shown, these address some of the shortcomings of the altruistic approach. They start from a different set of assumptions and move beyond utility considerations and the conceptualization of caring as a private good.

Chapter 4

CARING AS THE RESULT OF OTHER-REGARDING CHOICES

The conceptualization of caring within the economic concept of commitment

A concept that can incorporate utility arguments but does not assume that caring behavior must render utility to the care giver, thus avoiding some of the deficiencies of altruism pointed out above, is the concept of commitment as advanced by Amartya Sen. Although not proposed as an explicit conceptualization of caring services, it focuses on other-regarding rather than self-interested behavior and may be used to analyze and understand caring, especially in extreme dependency situations. (see also Nelson 1998)

Amartya Sen's concept of commitment

In his widely received article "Rational Fools: A Critique of the Behavioural Foundations of Economic Theory," first published in 1977, Sen conceptualizes other-regarding behavior within an (economic) concept of "commitment." Action motivated by commitment differs from that motivated by altruism in that the former is "non-egoistic" (Sen 1997: 92). In Sen's concept of commitment, considerations about another person's welfare precede considerations about the economic protagonist's own welfare. Sen conceptualizes commitment as a *counter*preferential choice in terms of "a person choosing an act that he [or she] believes will yield a lower level of personal welfare to him [or her] than an alternative that is also available to him [or her]" (Sen 1997: 92). With regard to the uncertainty concerning anticipated welfare, "commitment [...] involves choosing an action that yields a lower expected welfare than an available alternative" (Sen 1997: 93). By explicitly linking acts of commitment to a conscious *decrease* in the welfare of the protagonist, Sen rules out any possibility that the protagonist might be tempted by any self-interested welfare calculation. The point is that there is no *intended* maximization of one's own utility or welfare in actions motivated by commitment.[1] With his concept of "commitment," Sen

[1] The core assumptions of commitment certainly apply in the extreme case. The picture is less clear when a person's choice might coincide with the maximization of his/her anticipated personal welfare, even though this is neither intended nor the reason for the specific choice made. Yet it is feasible that in taking the welfare of another person as the motivation for action, one's own welfare may remain unaffected or might – unintentionally – even be

introduces a concept for action primarily motivated by the desire to increase the welfare of persons *other* than the economic protagonist her/himself.[2] This distinguishes commitment from altruism.[3]

Although featuring analytically separate utility functions (i.e. the same structure of utility functions underlying behavior based on self-interest), action based on commitment rather than on altruism would thus be *non-self-interested.* Commitment motivates one to act even where the action brings about no personal gain. It becomes possible to acknowledge the fact that an individual's actions may derive from considerations not covered – or at least not *fully* covered – by his/her own utility.[4] (Sen 1987: 41)

(1) Committed caring

The conceptualization of caring within the concept of commitment recognizes that caring behavior is not necessarily always identical with utility-maximizing behavior of the care *giver*. Rather, the utility of the care *receiver* may well matter to the care giver without assuming that the care giver maximizes his/her own utility through the performance of a caring service. For the intention of committed caring is to enhance – at least primarily – the utility and welfare of the care receiver. Caring conceptualized as behavior that primarily aims at enhancing the care receiver's welfare is *other*-interested behavior that does not derive from attached self-interest. It will be understood as *committed* caring.[5]

By breaking with the notion that a person makes contributions only if they add to his/her own utility, assumptions about utility return in the form of material or psychic income need not be made. Within the concept of committed caring, the care giver makes contributions to add to the care receiver's utility (and therefore parts with her/his wealth) even if this means a *decline* in the care giver's personal utility. Committed caring takes place even if no psychic income is to be expected either in the short, medium, or long term. Nor must long-term expectations of reciprocity be assumed. Committed caring behavior thereby provides security for the care receiver

---

enhanced by the action. For analytical purposes, therefore, it would seem advisable to conceptualize the extreme case to make sure that explicitly other-interested motivation is not confounded with self-interested motivations.

2 The comparison is between anticipated welfare levels. Acts going against self-interest because of a failure to foresee consequences are therefore excluded.

3 It should be noted that some authors understand "altruism" not in the Beckerian sense but similar to Sen's notion of "commitment". (e.g. Kirchgässner 2000: 176)

4 Sen affirms the existence of commitment; he does not put forward or discuss possible sources of commitment or the circumstances under which commitment might be created or fostered in people.

5 However, as Nelson points out, "commitment does not require, and in fact forbids [...] self-sacrifice" (Nelson 1996: 71, Fn. 8).

since care receivers (as well as society) can assume that caring services will be performed even where a sufficient degree of psychic or other income is not generated to attract the help of the care giver.

The scope of the concept

The concept of committed caring successfully explains the *other*-interested perspective, so important especially for the provision of caring for dependents. And it addresses some of the open questions about the concept of altruistic caring resulting from preferential choice as discussed above. It is equipped to meet the test case for any theory of caring in economics as conceptualized in Part I of this study: a caring situation characterized by the assumption that the care receiver would not be able to transfer resources back to the care giver at any point in time nor would there be much psychic income to the benefit of the care giver. The concept of commitment is therefore of special importance and relevance for studying situations involving the provision of care to dependents.

Committed caring is a concept that can deal with lifetime dependency of care receivers in a conceptual framework open to utility and welfare considerations; it operates on welfare and utility calculations, but shifts them to an other-interested rather than a self-interested perspective. As such it challenges economics by retaining one perspective familiar to economists while changing the other.

Altruism is, in some ways, an easier concept to analyze than commitment, since altruism can readily be incorporated into standard models by using the mechanism of interdependent utility functions. When a person's sense of well-being is psychologically dependent on someone else's welfare, all other things being equal, the awareness of the increase in the latter's welfare makes the former directly better off. The standard assumptions may therefore stay in place. But according to Sen, the introduction of commitment would require "that economic models be formulated in an essentially different way" (Sen 1997: 93) and "admitting behavior based on commitment would, of course, have far-reaching consequences on the nature of many economic models" (Sen 1997: 104).

By conceptualizing *other*-interested behavior, the concept of commitment – just as moral considerations – relies on a *connective* model of the individual. Commitment "violates the underlying separative individualism and hedonism" (Nelson 1996: 71) still present in the economic concept of altruism; it casts the individual, instead, as a *person-in-relation*, assuming care giver and care receiver as non separative (independent and disinterested) selves embedded in social relationships and institutional settings and capable of emphatic connections with others. No behavior committed to the need of the other would otherwise be possible.

Beyond a preference-based concept of commitment

Commitment as conceptualized by Sen reflects – as does altruism – a *preference-based theoretical* point of view. Altruism and commitment are conceptualized as personal preferences according to which an individual chooses to behave. In their analytical form they appear as options within the realm of personal choice. In such a framework, individual agents can choose the degree to which the welfare of others interferes with, enhances, or disadvantages their own personal welfare. (cf. also Nelson 1996: 70)

Commitment, however, "drives a wedge between personal choice and personal welfare" (Sen 1997: 94), whereas general economic theory relies on their identity. By asserting that actions may be taken quite apart from personal preference, and in this sense may be counterpreferential choices, the concept of commitment destroys the crucial assumption that choice always reflects preference and always is identical with enhancing the protagonist's welfare. (Sen 1997: 93)

Relinquishing the notion of preferential choice in economics has a far-reaching impact on economic theorizing. When the assumption is dropped that the economic protagonist maximizes his/her personal welfare, attention is directed to the question of other possible motivations for committed behavior, apart from self-interested utility maximization. Thus, a perspective is opened for the conception of an individual's behavior in terms of recognizing and respecting his/her ability to form goals, commitments, values, etc. – which is lost in a model of exclusively self-interested motivation, where individuals' behavior must be entirely geared to their own well-being measured in utility. (Sen 1987: 41; 1985)

Once the motive of welfare-oriented self-interest is relinquished, as it is in the case of caring, it becomes apparent that care givers themselves may have reasons for pursuing goals *other* than personal utility or individual self-interest. As has been shown above, these goals might still be utility and welfare-oriented in the sense that they aim at enhancing the utility and welfare of the care receiver as in the case of committed caring – they may, however, also derive from moral (such as responsibility, obligation, or duty) or other intrinsic motivations (such as affection or other emotional attachments).

This direction has been opened and prepared by Sen. His conceptual approach allows for the inclusion and discussion of considerations other than utility and welfare. He acknowledges that commitment is closely connected with moral considerations (Sen 1997: 93) and asserts that if the suffering of others "does not make you feel personally worse off, but you think it is wrong and you are ready to do something to stop it, it is a case of commitment" (Sen 1997: 92). In this sense the concept of commitment has a moral dimension.

Yet, the preference-theoretical point of view which constitutes the basis of Sen's concept of commitment is irreconcilable with the moral argument in the same theoretical concept since it is impossible to reduce moral motives which are not based on welfare calculations to an argument of utility considerations. Sen, however, although himself very well aware that moral categories are distinct from welfare considerations, and emphasizing the need to recognize this distinction (Sen 1987: 41), does not continue long this line of argumentation up to its final consequences when conceptualizing commitment. His attempt to include the preference-theoretical point of view and the moral perspective within the same conceptual framework thus necessarily results in inconsistency.

Chapter 5

CARING AS THE RESULT OF A CARING MOTIVATION

The conceptualization of caring derived from motivation

Another group of concepts of caring activities in economics centers on the crucial role played by motivation in bringing about a caring situation. These concepts highlight the need to distinguish *caring motivations* that reflect a caring attitude (and are in the focus of this section) from motives that do not. I call such motivation-derived caring concepts *two-fold* because they assume that two ingredients are needed for an effective caring situation: the provision of a caring service *and* a caring motivation on the part of the care giver. Examples of two-fold concepts of caring are found, for example in Himmelweit (1997, 1999), Folbre and Weisskopf (1998), Nelson (1998), and Tronto (1993). Himmelweit (1997) distinguishes between care as an activity and care as a motivation. Folbre and Weisskopf (1998) elaborate the difference between "caring services labor" as caring services performed without a caring motivation and "caring labor" to denote labor performed out of a caring motivation and therefore considered "both objectively and subjectively caring" (Folbre and Weisskopf 1998: 172). According to Nelson (1998) only the care service performed and the imparted feeling of being cared for, i.e. the instrumental and the communicative parts *taken together* constitute "real caring," in both paid and unpaid caring work. Tronto (1993) understands caring as "both a practice and a disposition" (Tronto 1993: 104), and confines references to care to situations where "both the activity and the disposition of care are present" (Tronto 1993: 105). Himmelweit calls it the "double characteristic of caring – that it is both motivation and activity" (Himmelweit 1999: 35).

Two-fold concepts distinguish two dimensions: i) the *instrumental*, namely the instrumental caring service performed (e.g. the actual diaper changed), and ii) the *communicative*, namely the cared-for feeling given. The communicative part is conceptualized as the non-commodifiable, non-transactable part whereas the instrumental service is looked upon as being commodifiable and transactable.[1] It is obvious that in the absence of the

---

[1] To identify whether or not a caring service is transactable or marketable, without suggesting that it always has to be marketed (Hill 1977: 317), the so-called *third-party criterion* (for its origins cf. Reid 1934: 11) is used. This criterion is fulfilled in cases where it would be conceivable to have an impersonal, unknown, unfamiliar, homogenous person perform the

communicative part, the instrumental part may still be performed. (cf. e.g. Tronto 1993: 105) In two-fold concepts of caring, however, the sole performance of an instrumental caring task absent a caring motivation cannot be considered caring since the communicative part, by definition, is crucial to the quality of the caring activity performed.

The concept of caring motivation

Special attention is therefore given to the classification of motivations that are considered caring. Folbre and Weisskopf propose a "typology of motives for care service labor" consisting of six motives and including both welfare considerations and moral considerations: "altruism" (affection), "a sense of responsibility" or obligation, "intrinsic enjoyment," "expectation of an informal quid pro quo" (reciprocity), "a well-defined and contracted for reward," fear of punishment stemming from "coercion" – ranged on a continuum from the most caring to the least caring. (Folbre and Weisskopf 1998: 174-179)

On this scale, affection and a sense of responsibility "most clearly qualify as caring" (Folbre and Weisskopf 1998: 179) and are considered more caring than enjoyment and informal reciprocity although these "are likely to contain some elements of caring" (Folbre and Weisskopf 1998: 179). The remaining two motives, contractual reward and fear are considered "uncaring" since individuals performing caring services only for such reasons are mainly concerned with their own welfare. The more caring the motivation in this context, the more the care giver is assumed to perform the caring service not in the interest of personal goals.[2]

Accordingly, the ideal caring motivation ensures that the caring service is *not instrumental* to the care giver's goals and that it is performed voluntarily. The assumption is that "people are prepared to do a great deal of work in providing care services to those whom they love or for whom they feel affection" (Folbre and Weisskopf 1998: 174). The ideal is for caring to flow from affection since "a genuine relationship of love or affection is completely voluntary, unburdened by any element of coercion" (Folbre and Weisskopf 1998: 174). Examples include romantic love in a successful intimate relationship and the affection parents ideally feel for their children.

caring service in question. A further precondition for the transactability of a service is that the service must be commodifiable in the sense that what one person performs for the benefit of another has to be operational, observable, quantifiable, and homogenous in physical terms, which also presupposes that it must be clearly distinguished from the benefit or utility that the consumer expects to derive from the service. (Hill 1977: 316)

[2] Note that neither here nor when "uncaring" behavior is discussed in following chapters "the line between caring and "un-caring" labour does not coincide with the line between non-market production and work for pay" (Badgett and Folbre 1999: 314).

The intrinsic motivation for the caring activity is looked upon as the defining characteristic. Emphasis is on the emotional investment that has been made or that has to be made in order to implement care. The objective of the caring activity, then, is not achieved by the satisfaction of an individual's needs but by the expression of an emotion: "to become sufficiently responsive, however, is to open oneself to the emotional attachments that characterize dependency work when well done" (Kittay 1999: 186). In two-fold concepts of caring, therefore, "the motives underlying the supply of care service labor have important implications for the quality of the services provided" (Folbre and Weisskopf 1998: 172).

Folbre and Weisskopf restrict their use of "caring labor" to caring services "performed out of a sense of affection or concern for others" (Folbre and Weisskopf 1998: 172; cf. also Folbre 1995: 75) – ideally characterized by the explicit absence of any extrinsic motivation such as "expectation of immediate pecuniary reward" (Folbre 1995: 75). Nancy Folbre even goes so far as to state as the "paradox of caring labor" that the only way to preserve the quality of caring is not to pay for it. (Folbre 1995: 87)[3] She thereby puts forward the ideal of a caring service as a one-way transfer, as a "labor grant," namely "the voluntary provision of personal services without a charge" (Boulding 1973: 30).

Caring services within this framework are perceived to be most caring when provided as "free or pure gifts" (Malinowski 1996 (1922)), that is, when they are one-way transfers of services for which nothing is expected in return (unlike reciprocated one-way transfers). Pure gift giving constitutes the "solidarity extreme" (Sahlins 1996 (1974): 31) of human interaction. According to Marshall Sahlins, a good pragmatic indication of pure gift giving is a sustained one-way flow where "failure to reciprocate does not cause the giver [...] to stop giving: the goods [or services] move one way, in favor of the have-not, for a very long period" (Sahlins 1974: 194; 1996: 31-32). Sahlins identifies assistance and need as the most common rationale behind pure gift giving. The expectation of returns – if any – is correspondingly indefinite: "reciprocation is formally unconditional, it may be left until a need precipitates it, it bears no necessary equivalence to the

[3] Monetary reward is commonly referred to as an extrinsic motivation, i.e. an incentive for behavior applied from outside the person considered; the assumption is that people change their actions because they are induced to do so by an external intervention. Most motivations for caring fall into the range of intrinsic motivations – at least the most caring ones – and motivate the care giver "to perform an activity when one receives no apparent reward except the activity itself" (Frey 1997: 13). Economic theory generally takes extrinsic motivation to be relevant for behavior, and the established practice is to attribute changes in behavior to independently observable changes in constraints. On the definition of intrinsic motivation cf. also Kirchgässner 2000: 180. As Frey has pointed out, however, the distinction between intrinsic and extrinsic motivation is not always clear-cut. (Frey 1997: 14)

initial gift, and the material flow can be unbalanced in favor of one side or the other for a long time" (Sahlins 1974: 206).[4] As the norm of reciprocity "cannot apply with full force in relations with children, old people, or with those who are mentally or physically handicapped" (Gouldner 1996 (1960): 66), pure gifts play an important role as regards the provision of caring services. Irene van Staveren considers gift giving as the allocation mechanism in the economic-value domain of care.[5] (van Staveren 1999: 46)

The assumption of nothing being given in return, of no future reciprocation for the labor grant, is a crucial aspect with regard to the performance of caring services for dependents since, in the most severe cases of dependency, no return can be expected owing to the dependent's age, or mental, or physical health. In these cases it is likely that some of the dependent care receivers will never be able to reciprocate what is done for them. In the case of care for very small children, for example, "the expectation of a direct material return or service is unseemly. At best it is implicit. The material side of the transaction is repressed by the social: reckoning of debts outstanding cannot be overt and is typically left out of account. [...] The counter is not stipulated by time, quantity, or quality: the expectation of reciprocity, if any, is indefinite" (Sahlins 1996: 31).[6] Caring services performed from motivations which do not involve the expectation of returns are thus provided within gift relationships.

Caring motivations so conceptualized reduce the risk which exchange might entail for the care receiver. The more caring the motivation, the less the care receiver has to worry about eventual expectations of returns. This is a great comfort and security for care receivers, especially for dependents who have nothing to offer in return (particularly in the short term) and who otherwise must fear the loss of all caring attention.[7]

The distinction between caring motives and non-caring motives is not the same as the distinction between non-market and market activities, though the dichotomies are related. Most self-interested behavior in Western societies takes place in the market with the reward taking the form of

---

[4] Because of this, pure gift giving is sometimes also referred to as "generalized [or indefinite] reciprocity" (Sahlins 1974: 191; 1996: 31). The term, however, has not been adopted in this study so that gifts may clearly be distinguished from mutual grants and reciprocal relationships.

[5] According to van Staveren, besides the "domain of care," the other two economic-value domains are the "domain of freedom," with exchange as allocation mechanism, and the "domain of justice," with distributive rules as allocation mechanism. (van Staveren 1999: 46)

[6] Not all systems of reciprocity expect reciprocal returns from the person benefited by the labor grant proper. In family-based or societal systems of reciprocity, someone else – or even a future generation – may provide the return.

[7] The only other way to ensure that care receivers who have nothing to offer in return receive at least the instrumental services needed would be coercing care givers into care giving, albeit the expense of quality.

monetary compensation. But narrowly self-interested behavior can also take place outside the labor market with non-monetary rather than monetary rewards. And caring services may sometimes be remunerated, even if they are provided for reasons that do not chiefly involve self-interest.

Nor is the provision of caring services the only way in which caring motives may be expressed. Other human activities may be carried out with a caring end, yet they generally do not constitute caring services as understood in this study. (Tronto 1993: 104; Biesecker 1996) Out of affection or concern one could also make a gift in money or kind, or one could provide another person with a continuing income or continuing access to some purchased services. This "caring provision" (Folbre and Weisskopf 1998: 173), i.e. "the supplying of money or resources for the acquisition of care services from a third party [...] is rarely a perfect substitute for the actual performance of caring labor" (Folbre and Weisskopf 1998: 173).

Focusing on the importance and role of the caring motivation or making it the defining characteristic of caring activities may run the danger of individualizing and privatizing caring, as well as sentimentalizing it. Thinking of caring primarily in motivational terms may lead to the idea that caring is entirely individual, and that no generalized statements can reasonably be made on the effectiveness of any given caring situation or on the failure to achieve a satisfactory level in caring activities.[8] This type of analysis may further encourage the use of certain stereotypes or prejudices in approaching topics such as the roles within society's division of labor. Gender roles and the idea of the "predisposition" of women for caring activities would be reinforced; the assumption of caring motivation in women and the assignment of caring activities to women would be taken for granted and assured.

Two-fold concepts of caring call attention to the importance of a caring motivation as a defining characteristic of caring activities. But even though dispositions and emotions are an essential part of caring, they constitute caring behavior only in combination with the performance of an instrumental caring activity.

---

[8] To avoid such one-sided emphasis, caring has also been conceptualized in terms of a "practice." (e.g. Ruddick 1987: 132-133; Tronto 1993: 104 and 118) Different caring practices and their goals shape demands on the care giver in different ways. Love, fostering growth, and training for social acceptance, for example, guide maternal practice. Caring for the frail elderly, in turn, is guided by a concern and respect as well as fostering self-sufficiency and self-esteem with respect to the encountered disintegration of social acceptability. Caring for dependents requires involvement in each aspect of these respective practices. (Kittay 1999: 33)

The concept of integrative product

Two-fold concepts of caring stress the importance of the presence of a caring motivation for the provision of a caring service. Only a caring motivation, so the argument, can ensure the production of something felt to be essential for and characteristic of successful and effective caring. Nancy Folbre conceptualizes this distinctive feature of real caring services as the production of a "joint product." (Folbre 1995; Folbre and Weisskopf 1998) The joint product is distinct from the instrumental aspects of the caring service. It constitutes the communicative dimension of caring and conceptualizes the personal relation which results from the person-to-person interaction in the provision of caring services. The joint product arises if an instrumental caring service is performed with a caring motivation. Its production has its source in and is ensured by the caring motivation involved. The presence of the joint product, therefore, distinguishes real caring services from non-caring services.

The joint product on the care receiver's side is "the confirmation to the care recipient that someone cares about him or her" (Folbre and Weisskopf 1998: 180), which Folbre and Weisskopf call "caring" (Folbre and Weisskopf 1998: 192). The joint product on the care giver's side is the positive satisfaction the care giver derives from giving someone else the confirmation that they care about them. Folbre and Weisskopf call this joint product the "warm glow" (Folbre and Weisskopf 1998: 181).[9] Caring and the warm glow are produced at the same time, uno actu, according to the assumption. They are two sides of the same coin and are assumed to enhance the quality of the care service in an important respect. Caring and warm glow have intrinsic value and evade commodification (e.g. Folbre 1995); they are intangible and non-transactable except within the caring relationship they are created in.

The concept of joint product makes clear that in talking about caring services one is talking about services which provide "products" of a special kind. In part, the products of caring are conventional services. But (joint) "products" of a different sort and quality are also simultaneously created. They do not bring about a change in the condition of the care receiver as the definition of a service requires. (Hill 1977; Hawrylyshyn 1977) Rather, they may be conceptualized as the creation of something different that involves both care receiver and care giver: the care provided is inseparable from the caring relationship created for and through it. (Himmelweit 1999: 29)

---

[9] Cf. also Andreoni (1989), who includes the pleasure of giving (a "warm glow effect") in the utility function. (Fehr and Schmidt 2000)

This qualitative difference in the provision of caring services[10] as opposed to non-caring services is made visible with the help of Margaret Jane Radin's concept of "work." Radin distinguishes "work" from "labor" asserting that "it is possible to think of work as always containing a noncommodified human element; and to think of the fully commodified version as labor" (Radin 1996: 105).[11] Ideally then, the provision of caring services is the performance of caring work. Even if it is paid for and performed in a market context, caring work is characterized by and retains an important non-commodifiable dimension.[12]

Caring work is relational and integrative. As Himmelweit puts it, "relationships matter not only in the allocation of caring; the process of caring is itself the development of a relationship." (Himmelweit 1999: 29) The confirmation that someone cares, and the warm glow felt in the performance of caring work are evidence to care giver and care receiver alike that they have successfully established a caring relationship with a fellow human being. And that represents a successful situating of themselves with regard to others. The concept of caring work therefore aptly reflects the successful establishment of a relationship between the care giver and the care receiver.

The scope of the concept

The public dimension of caring

The concept of joint product describes one of the essential characteristics and main tasks of caring activities as outlined in Chapter 1 of this study. It

[10] In economics, the terms "good" and "service" are commonly used synonymously for "economic good" and "economic service." But even though the concepts of goods and services are taken from economics, a conceptual difference can be made between goods and economic goods as well as between services and economic services. Although the economic concept of a service takes the commodifiability (transactability, marketability) of these specific economic goods for granted, it is possible to describe the nature of a caring service independent of its possible commodifiability. By contrast, a service's commodifiability (transactability, marketability) must be identified specifically for every given service.

[11] Radin stresses the importance of the category of items which are inalienable by sale and are therefore located outside the market, but which might still be transferred by gift and could thus be objects of social interaction. (Radin 1996: 18) Note, however, that alienation is not necessarily associated with pay.

[12] In the following, Radin's distinction will be applied when using the terms "work" and "labor" in this study. One should be aware, however, that other authors use the terms labor and work differently. Folbre and Weisskopf's "caring labor" mentioned above would be caring work according to Radin whereas Tronto's "caring work" (Tronto 1993: 105) would be caring labor in Radin's sense.

indicates that the care giver has successfully positioned her/himself in the world and society, in this case in relation to another individual. The joint product defines the connection made. In this sense the joint product can more specifically be called *integrative product*.

While Becker's concept of household commodities helps us to more aptly describe the personal, non-transactable part of caring, the concept itself, as *household* commodities, prevents us from taking the discussion to the societal level. Since the concept does not differentiate between the communicative dimension of caring and the instrumental performance of a caring service, the non-transactability argument referring to the communicative part is superimposed upon the instrumental part. The entire product of caring is thus considered non-transactable, with the result that the exclusive conceptualization of caring as a household commodity confines this concept of caring to the informal, unpaid, private sphere of the economy.[13] The concept of joint or integrative product by contrast conveys the essence of the communicative part, that is so intrinsically interwoven with the instrumental tasks of caring and takes the concept of caring beyond the family, the household, the neighborhood, and the workplace. Since two-fold concepts of caring distinguish the transactable and non-transactable parts of caring, they can account for the fact that the instrumental service may be transactable and taken to the market (and be positively stimulated by pecuniary compensation like other market activities) or the public sphere, and may be enforceable through coercion resulting in alienated caring labor. By stating that motives crucially matter in the provision of real caring two-fold concepts emphasize that "precisely because it focuses on motives, caring labor [Radin's "work" (see Chapter 5, Note 12)] can apply to both men and women, the market and the family, production and reproduction" (Folbre 1995: 76). The joint or integrative product may be produced independent of the family context, and it may be produced for strangers. The integrative products of caring are individually and personally generated but the structures they enhance are beneficial to the whole of society. Through their inherently ethical nature they are situated within the societal and public dimensions of caring situations.

The two-fold supply function

With the help of two-fold concepts of caring, the demand and supply of care services could possibly be specified and policy tasks reformulated. Conceptualizing caring as consisting of both instrumental and communicative dimensions, and identifying "real caring" as caring work, are

---

[13] Consequently, Becker's concept cannot account for that part of caring services that can be taken to the market; it must hold that formal and informal caring products are fundamentally different.

helpful analytical tools toward better differentiation and more precision in the discussion on the social organization of caring situations and the provision of caring services.

Two-fold concepts of caring enable the analysis to make clear that a reduction in the provision of instrumental caring labor does not necessarily imply an overall reduction in caring motivations, and that a decline in the provision of instrumental caring labor does not necessarily imply a decrease in caring services motivated by caring motivations.[14] The relative decline in "real caring" appears as a relative decline in the production of the integrative product. The whole project of ensuring the performance of caring activities can be understood as two-fold: one task is to ensure the presence of caring motivations and the provision of the instrumental part of caring activities; the other task is to ensure the generation of the integrative product – and, ideally, to "package" the two by encouraging caring motivations. It also becomes clear that, while coercive and discriminating social situations may ensure the performance of the instrumental parts of caring, their lack of caring motivations make them unable to generate the integrative product. Caring by compulsion does not generate "real caring."

The introduction of moral motives

The range of caring motivations discussed in this chapter explicitly takes the concept of caring to motivations that can deal with asymmetric dependency situations without assuming a return from the care receiver. Affection, duty, moral obligation, and responsibility are understood not to be based on an altruistic utility calculus.

The role of moral motivations in the provision of caring has been widely discussed, most prominently in the work of political philosophers. Here, caring is often viewed as an attempt to "meet the other morally" (Noddings 1984: 4), as "more than simply a passing interest or fancy but instead the acceptance of some form of burden" (Tronto 1993: 103, see also: 125-155), and the ethics of care are seen as a moral orientation (Sevenhuijsen 1998: 36-68).[15] This argument assumes its full weight with regard to dependency work. Kittay argues that the dependency worker – even if he/she refuses to undertake affective involvement for the dependent – has a distinctive moral obligation. She further argues that "the moral features of dependency work

[14] But "it suggests the need to explore the substitutability between different forms of expressing care (purchasing things for people versus doing things for them) and between different motives for supplying care services (self-interest versus care)" (Folbre and Weisskopf 1998: 174).

[15] For theoretical approaches to caring ethics see e.g. Bowden 1997; Sevenhuijsen 1998; Tronto 1993. Cf. also the debate on an ethics of care following Carol Gilligan's widely received studies on women's conceptions of self and morality (e.g. Gilligan 1982).

[...] include both the moral responsibilities of the dependency worker to [the care receiver], and the moral obligation of those who stand outside to the dependency relationship to support such a relation" (Kittay 1999: 50).

Although the preference-based concept of committed caring appears interrelated with caring services motivated by moral obligations or feelings of duty, and while commitment and obligation are frequently treated as either intermingled or as substitutes in the presentation of caring motives, there is an important difference between the two. (see Chapter 4)

This distinction is lost, however, if behavior motivated by affection, duty, obligation, and responsibility is modeled as altruistic behavior, as is done, for example, by Folbre and Weisskopf (1998).[16] Though critical of a pure utility approach, the authors cast their concept of caring work as altruistic behavior ideally motivated by affection.[17] The conceptualization of affection within the concept of altruism, injects emotion into the world of utility arguments. In their use of altruism, however, Folbre and Weisskopf depart from the concept of economic altruism as outlined in Chapter 3, which assumes a return of material or psychic income to the care giver for the service performed. Although they conceptualize altruism as positively interdependent utility, suggesting that the utility of the care receiver matters to the care giver, they simultaneously argue that "care service labor motivated by altruism does not necessarily require any reward or quid pro quo, other than evidence that the cared-for person benefits from it. It may even be undertaken completely independently of the response of the cared-for person" (Folbre and Weisskopf 1998: 174) as might be the case when care is provided to a comatose relative. In doing so they apply a concept of altruism which is different from Becker's concept since Folbre and Weisskopf do not expect a reward. The assumption that affective caring work may be undertaken completely independent of the response of the cared-for person within the economic concept of altruism leaves the question of return conceptually unresolved. Does caring work seek a return or not?

The apparent contradiction in the argumentation may be explained as the result of a precipitate equating of the motive of affection with the concept of altruism. In their conceptualization of affection Folbre and Weisskopf go beyond self-interest narrowly interpreted but they also go beyond pure utility calculations. Rather, they call the utility approach into question and emphasize the contrast of caringly motivated work and the motivations for work characteristic of homo oeconomicus. (Folbre and Weisskopf 1998:

---

[16] Cf. also Kirchgässner who conceptualizes altruistic and moral actions as identical and uses the terms synonymously. (Kirchgässner 2000: 176)

[17] In Folbre and Weisskopf (1998) the question as to why affection is equated with altruism and not, for example, with intrinsic enjoyment, or conceptualized in its own way, remains open.

173) It is the notion of affection which the authors conceptualize – not economic altruism. To take full account of the notion of affection, Folbre and Weisskopf depart from the economic concept of altruism by changing the assumptions that are definitive for the concept of altruism itself. And, in fact, they are forced to do so. The conceptualization of affective behavior as altruistic behavior, however, confines the notion of affection to self-interested utility considerations, which are not considered reconcilable with the conception of caring affection as put forward by the authors. The attempt by Folbre and Weisskopf to treat the motive of affection as part of the economic concept of altruism leads to the same inconsistency uncovered in relation to Sen. (see Chapter 4) The conceptualization of affection as behavior that does not expect a return within the economic concept of altruism remains at least unsatisfactory, if not contradictory and unresolved.

The impact of fairness models and Crowding Theory

Although two-fold concepts allow for a range of possible motivations for caring, including extrinsic motives, they clearly stress the importance of intrinsic motivation. And while not all intrinsic motivations are necessarily *caring* motivations, most *caring* motivations as conceptualized by two-fold concepts of caring are *intrinsic* motivations which are understood as a precondition for the communicative aspect and the production of the integrative product essential for qualities of "real caring" as distinct from the mere performance of the instrumental activity.

Highlighting the importance of intrinsic motivation for economically relevant human behavior is not new to economic theory. Nor is it singular or exclusive to the analysis of caring activities. Studies by economists in other areas such as environmental behavior, the siting of hazardous facilities, and the fulfillment of labor contracts have indicated that economically relevant behavior can be motivated intrinsically and extrinsically. Recent findings of experimental economists have confirmed this. By emphasizing and studying intrinsic motivations, two-fold concepts may thus both rely on and feed back into the works of economists who empirically demonstrate that intrinsic motivations are important determinants of human behavior and that the reasons behind the economic protagonist's action encompass a much larger variety of motivations than just self-interest. (Kirchgässner 2000: 157-200; Frey 1997: 118; Fehr and Schmidt 2000) Such economists acknowledge limits to the explanatory power of the assumption of unattached self-interest with regard to certain spheres in the economy and society (Kirchgässner 2000: 222) and they conceptualize economic subjects with a more refined motivational structure.[18]

---

[18] Yet general (mainstream) economic reasoning continues to concentrate on and work with only a fraction of these motivations and to assume unattached self-interested utility or welfare

Two of these lines of research are of particular interest for the discussion here: i) theories of fairness as developed by recent research in experimental economics and ii) the systematic relationship between extrinsic and intrinsic motivations as put forward by Crowding Theory (as developed by Bruno S. Frey). These theoretical approaches do not explicitly treat or examine caring activities; they therefore do not constitute conceptual approaches to caring in economics as such. Yet, their main elements and findings are of relevance for the analysis and conceptualization of caring activities in economics.[19]

Caring and experimental theories of fairness

In recent years, experimental economists have gathered evidence that systematically refutes the self-interest hypothesis and suggests that many people are strongly motivated by a variety of altruistic motives and concerns of fairness and reciprocity, and are willing to reward or punish other individuals at considerable cost to themselves.[20] Fehr and Schmidt argue that "it is not only necessary but also very promising for mainstream economics to take the presence of other-regarding preferences into account" (Fehr und Schmidt 2000) since people differ with regard to how self-interested or fair-minded they are and this is of important economic consequence. Experiments show that people are not always guided by their own absolute advantages. For if the distribution undertaken within the group violates their norms of fairness they readily accept a considerable reduction of their own material advantage.

Fairness models in experimental economics work within a rational choice framework and seek to explain that many people not only seek to maximize their own material income but are also concerned about social comparisons, fairness, and the desire to reciprocate. These fairness considerations are not restricted to personal interactions with others, as in the family, workplace, or among neighbors, friends, and strangers but also shape the behavior of people in important economic domains. Fehr and Schmidt distinguish two main approaches: (1) the assumption of social preferences and (2) the assumption of intention-based reciprocity. (Fehr and Schmidt 2000) The starting point of both is the positing of rather specific assumptions as to the utility functions of the players.

---

considerations as the economic protagonist's motivation for action. On the prevalence of the assumption of self-interest cf. Kirchgässner 2000: 61; also Fehr and Schmidt 2000; Frey 1997: 123.

[19] The following discussion will confine itself to the main arguments of each approach and does not pretend to be a comprehensive presentation.

[20] For an overview see Fehr and Schmidt 2000. The authors present, analyze, and discuss theories of fairness and reciprocity. In their paper, fairness or fair-mindedness seems to be understood as the opposite of self-interest. The notion of fairness or fair-mindedness, however, is not developed in any further detail.

(1) Social preferences

Models of social preferences assume that at least some decision makers not only have preferences about allocations of material outcomes for themselves but that they may additionally care about how much material resources are allocated to others; their utility function not only depends on their own material payoff but also on how much the other players receive. Special forms of this altruistic behavior are conceptualized as quasi-maximin preferences, relative income and envy, inequity aversion, and altruism and spitefulness.[21] Of special interest in the context of caring are the concepts of quasi-maximin preferences and inequity aversion.[22]

Quasi-maximin preferences can explain positive acts of care givers toward care receivers by assuming that the care giver cares about the well-being of the care receiver all the more so if the care receiver is worse off than the care giver. According to the concept of *inequity aversion*, a care giver would be altruistic toward a potential care receiver if the care receiver's material payoff is below an equitable benchmark[23] but would feel envy if the material payoff of the care receiver exceeded that level.[24] Accordingly, if dependent care receivers fall below this equitable benchmark – which they very likely do – they may expect the performance of one-way transfers of caring services. Thus caring behavior toward dependents may occur within this concept. On the other hand, there is the assumption that an altruistic player feels more altruistic toward another altruist than toward a spiteful person, as featured in the concept of altruism, and that spitefulness expects returns from the care receiver and may lead individuals to establish caring relations only or primarily with those who can reciprocate.

(2) Intention-based reciprocity

Models of social preferences assume that players are concerned only about the distributional consequences of their own acts and not about the intentions of other players. By contrast, models of intention-based reciprocity[25] start from the observation that human behavior is often a

---

[21] For a short presentation of each of these see Fehr and Schmidt 2000.

[22] The relative income and envy concept is based on the hypothesis that subjects are concerned not only about the absolute amount of money they receive but also about their relative standing compared to others. They suffer if they get less than the others but are indifferent if there are better off. (Fehr and Schmidt 2000). This concept is not of relevance in the context of caring activities.

[23] Most experiments assume an equal monetary payoff for all players as equitable allocation.

[24] Unlike quasi-maximin preferences, models of inequity aversion work with a utility function which can rationalize positive and negative actions toward other players. They also work on the assumption that individuals are heterogeneous. (Fehr and Schmidt 2000)

[25] For an overview of current approaches see Fehr and Schmidt 2000.

reaction to the (expected) intentions of other people. If applied to caring behavior this would mean that if care givers feel treated kindly by care receivers, they will want to return the kindness. If, however, they feel treated badly, they will want to hurt the care receiver even if costly to them personally. In this approach, the care giver's interpretation of the care receiver's behavior is crucial. According to this theory, care givers would also not undertake kind actions unless care receivers have shown their kind intentions. This contrasts with models of inequity aversion according to which care givers behave altruistically towards care receivers irrespective of their intentions.

The experimental situation and caring for dependents

Studies of fairness offer empirical evidence of variations in altruism which may help to shed more light on the distinctions within altruistic motives behind caring and therefore also provide interesting insights for understanding caring activities. But it is important to note that the insights from these theories have not been gained on the basis of experiments in care or dependency settings modeling the provision of caring activities or dependency services. Although some of the motivations named above may move people to care for others, one cannot simply transfer the concepts of experimental economics to the understanding of caring situations. For the concepts of specific forms of altruism in experimental economics are based on situations of human interaction which are quite different from typical caring and especially dependency situations as discussed in this study.

Experimental economics relies on experimental evidence concerning human decision-making.[26] In "clean" experimental studies, real subjects make decisions with real monetary consequences in carefully controlled laboratory settings. In such experiments, subjects do not know one another's identities, they interact anonymously, and sometimes even the experimenter is unable to observe their individual choices. (Fehr and Schmidt 2000) Behavior is observed to determine the willingness or unwillingness to take or forsake material payoffs – not with respect to performing a caring activity. The starting positions of the players are assumed to be equal in terms of their capabilities to decide and act. Players in experimental situations respond to the reaction (intended or actual) of the other players. Their behavior toward others is influenced by the behavior of others toward

---

[26] Experimental evidence has been collected in the field of imperfect labor contracts, inappropriate income tax schedules, tax evasion, compliance with contractual obligations, organizational rules, law in general, public support for the regulation of private industries, the solution of collective-action problems, and public support for the welfare state. (Fehr and Schmidt 2000)

them. It is assumed that other players can autonomously choose their own actions and be cooperative, benevolent, reciprocating, etc.

The conditions for such an experimental set-up, however, are not met in most caring situations. Only in some dependency situations can the dependent, as the person who benefits from the fair behavior of the others, act as a player. Dependent care receivers with limited or no autonomy would have to be considered "dummy players" in such models, i.e. players who are unable to affect distribution by their actions or have no choice to make, and yet are affected by the action or non-action of others.[27]

The hypotheses of experimental economics still have to be tested in caring situations, especially in caring situations involving dependents. It is likely that they may have to be reconsidered from a dependency point of view. It is also likely that the dependency perspective will, in turn, provide insights for these theories and suggestions for the further set-up of experimental situations where the assumptions of autonomy and dependency for the care receiver will be of crucial importance.

Intrinsic motivation and Crowding Theory

Ever since Richard M. Titmuss' study on blood donation (Titmuss 1973), the remuneration of intrinsically motivated behavior has been subject to critical scrutiny. Titmuss argued that paying individuals to perform social services for sick and disadvantaged members of society risks undermining these individuals' motivation for doing so.[28] (Titmuss 1973: 246) His hypotheses have been further tested, and the insights taken from psychological research have been transferred to the analysis of economic actions. The most common hypotheses tested and the most common results reveal that commodification and pricing of intrinsically motivated behavior encourage profit-maximizing behavior and "crowd-out" what had been an intrinsic motivation to give altruistically, thus leading to a decline in quality of the

---

[27] On the limits to altruism in this respect see also Chapter 5.

[28] From the study of the private market in blood in the United States vis-à-vis the entirely voluntary blood donorship in Great Britain, Titmuss concluded that "the commercialization of blood and donor relationships represses the expression of altruism, erodes the sense of community, lowers scientific standards, limits both personal and professional freedoms, sanctions the making of profits in hospitals and clinical laboratories, legalizes hostility between doctor and patient, subjects critical areas of medicine to the laws of the marketplace, places immense social costs on those least able to bear them – the poor, the sick, and the inept" (Titmuss 1970: 246). He found that it increases the danger of unethical behavior in various sectors of medical science and practice and results "in situations in which proportionally more and more blood is supplied by the poor, the unskilled, the unemployed, African Americans and other low income groups and categories of exploited human populations of high blood yielders" (Titmuss 1970: 246). For reflections on the descriptive and prescriptive issues raised by Titmuss' evidence and assertions see Arrow 1972.

good or service provided. Bruno Frey (1997) showed that there is a tendency toward the same outcome when regulations and mandates are introduced in areas of voluntary and charitable work. By paying for intrinsically motivated services, so the argument, "the relationship based on benevolence is basically transformed; if it survives at all, it is then a commercial one which all the people involved interpret quite differently" (Frey 1997: 8).[29]

The main elements of Crowding Theory

Crowding Theory (featuring both "crowding-*out*" and "crowding-*in*") takes account of these findings and establishes a systematic relationship between intrinsic and extrinsic motivations. Crowding-out Theory takes a well-defined and particular psychological effect, namely the "hidden cost of reward," which is important in economic affairs, generalizes it, and integrates it into economic theory by modeling it as a "substitution effect where individuals reduce the motivation under their control (intrinsic motivation) when an external intervention by pricing or regulating confronts them with an extrinsic motivation"(Frey 1997: 121).

The main hypothesis is that under identifiable conditions (1) monetary incentives (and the striving for profit they might inspire) as well as (2) other interventions external to a particular individual (regulations with mandates, rules, punishments) undermine and crowd-out intrinsic motivation (Crowding-*out* Effect). That is, economic subjects under identifiable conditions react in the opposite direction of the Price Effect – supply is reduced, and an activity is undertaken less intensively. A monetary payment or a strict mandate results in the reduction of the corresponding activity. Under some (rather rare) conditions (3) external intervention bolsters intrinsic motivation (Crowding-*in* Effect). (Frey 1997: 118-119)

The Crowding Effect appears under two psychological conditions formulated in terms of subjective perception: external intervention crowds-*out* intrinsic motivation if the individuals affected perceive the intervention to be of controlling influence. In that case, self-determination, self-esteem, and the possibility for expression suffer, and the individuals react by reducing their intrinsic motivation in the activity controlled.[30] On the other hand, external intervention crowds-*in* intrinsic motivation if the individuals

---

[29] Cf. also Boulding who argues that even if paid labor might be considered more efficient in the technical sense, something is lost with respect to the integrative system in the move from voluntary to paid labor. (Boulding 1973: 32)

[30] According to Frey, this behavior is due to the "Overjustification Effect," expressing that individuals feel overjustified if they maintain their intrinsic motivation when confronted with (additional) outside incentives. Individuals, so Frey's argument, react by reducing the intrinsic motivation under their control since, in the presence of outside incentives, intrinsic motivation seems unnecessary. (Frey 1997: 17)

concerned perceive it as supportive. In that case, self-esteem is fostered and individuals feel that they are given more freedom to act, thus enlarging self-determination.

The basic idea of Crowding Theory is that there are situations in which intrinsic motivation is central, and in which external intervention perceived to be of controlling influence has a strong crowding-out effect. If, by contrast, intrinsic motivation influences behavior little or not at all, there can be no crowding-out effect. (Frey 1997: 26) Crowding Theory deals with the relationship between extrinsic and intrinsic motivating forces and seeks to identify the conditions under which each is appropriate. (Frey 1997: 2-3) It uncovers the conditions or areas in which the Price Effect guides human behavior, and the conditions where Crowding Effects are to be expected. (Frey 1997: 120)

Empirical evidence, for example, has shown that additionally compensating employees, in particular managers, for tasks generally viewed as part of the job (so-called performance payment) is likely to replace self-determined by outside determined work, and therewith reduce personal involvement, creativity, and effort. Another finding was that paying a community to host hazardous facilities has the disadvantage that the monetary offer crowds-out the citizens' motivation to act on behalf of the common good. And other communities also become unwilling to host such facilities without remuneration in the future. As a consequence, it often becomes impossible to undertake locally hosted projects of benefit to society as a whole. Similarly, unfortunate spillover effects are to be expected when a community is forced by central government to accept a locally unwanted installation. (Frey 1997: 11)

Frey concluded from his studies that the political application of monetary rewards must be carefully administrated since intrinsically motivated actions seemed to follow different rules from extrinsically motivated actions.

But this careful observation has often been applied and translated into policy recommendations with no attention paid to its specific circumstances. What has remained in many instances is the rather crude statement that one should not monetarily reward intrinsically motivated behavior, or even shorter: do not pay intrinsically motivated behavior (in general). Such an understanding, however, besides being an inadequate simplification, obscures rather than clarifying the situations analyzed. And its application to the provision of caring may serve as a problematic example in this regard.

The transferability to caring situations

Does Crowding Theory apply to the study of caring activities? If so, to what extent? This question will be tackled by discussing two separate issues, namely, (1) the possibility of transferring empirical observation from Crowding Theory to the provision of caring activities, and (2) the possibility of transferring the political conclusions of Crowding Theory to caring situations.

(1) Empirical observations from Crowding Theory are not derived from dependency situations, nor do they explicitly deal with caring activities. Still, Frey refers to the importance of intrinsic motivation in the family context stating that "the behavior in an extended family tends to be different from a nuclear family because in the latter intrinsic motivation in the form of altruism is more important and family members are careful not to crowd it out" (Frey 1997: 27). Similar to concepts of caring activities which take caring motivations to reflect the relatedness between the two individuals involved, Crowding Theory considers motivation to be an indication of the kind of relationship in question. Frey, more particularly, also refers to altruism as "the extent to which individuals are prepared to share funds with others, which is a particular kind of intrinsic motivation" (Frey 1997: 15) and observes that "the subjects' altruism of giving to other persons was undermined when they were *forced* to share with another person" (Frey 1997: 15; emphasis in the original). He also alludes to the possible crowding-out of intrinsic motivation for charitable work.

However, none of his examples are taken from the realm of care. Furthermore, Frey hardly has caring activities in mind when formulating his typology of activities perceived to be of intrinsic interest to their performers and relating the degree to which a task is more interesting (more complex or conceptual and less dull or repetitive) to the degree of intrinsic motivation to perform well and the perceived self-determination and self-evaluation of the actor. As he finds: "it seems fair to state that the liberal professions such as lawyers, architects, doctors or artists, as well as academics tend to consider their jobs more intrinsically interesting than less educated employees" (Frey 1997: 28).

As decidedly personal relationships, caring relationships are expected to be prone to crowding-out. In terms of the more interesting, more complex or conceptual and less dull and repetitive part, things look different. How "interesting" are many caring tasks from this perspective? After all, they are more often than not the job of the less and least educated. What kind of and how much self-determination and self-evaluation is there to be crowded-out? And not all caring activities are complex and conceptual; in fact, they may be rather dull and repetitive – at least from the instrumental point of view. It is only by their communicative aspect and the creation of the integrative product that these activities may appear more "interesting."

Dependency relationships are not intrinsically motivated because they are personal relationships; nor are the intrinsically motivated because they are specifically "interesting" in Frey's sense. The relevance of intrinsic motivation in the provision of dependency services originates from another source: such jobs are said to be intrinsically motivated because they must be performed even in the absence of any extrinsic motivation, since their non-performance could have life-threatening consequences for the care receiver. They are also performed with an eye to the importance of the integrative product.

The main characteristic of dependency services is that they are activities that answer a basic need or respond to an unavoidable dependence in terms of very survival – not that they are complex and interesting. Intrinsic motivations in these cases might react quite differently to external intervention. Although they fall under the broader range of intrinsically motivated activities, they are distinct from the other activities identified by Frey as prone to crowding-out. This does not mean, however, that care givers are immune to external intervention. There are circumstances in which crowding-out effects may take place. As the discussion in Chapter 7 will show, these are likely to occur as the result of inadequate (little) pay and the stiffening of rules and regulations. Crowding observations and hypotheses, therefore, must be carefully studied to determine the extent to which they apply to caring situations.

(2) Above all, however, the policy conclusions drawn from crowding-out theory have been transferred to caring situations. This has unfortunately been done in a crude and rather generalized manner as in the case of Folbre's "paradox of caring labor" mentioned above by which "the only way to preserve the true value of this work is not to pay for it" (Folbre 1995: 87). Folbre's paradox reflects the crowding-out argument, namely, that by the introduction of extrinsic incentives the integrative relationship is placed in question and very likely destroyed or at least substantially transformed.

Folbre and Weisskopf argue that although "increasing the wage offered for provision of caring services could have several positive effects, eliciting higher levels of skill, reducing levels of worker turnover, and enhancing opportunities for workers to develop a genuine caring relationship with clients" (Folbre and Weisskopf 1998: 181), it cannot elicit a greater supply of "real caring" and "may even have a crowding-out effect by eroding the kind of values which underlie the motivation for caring labor" (Folbre and Weisskopf 1998: 181). The profit motive threatens to replace the caring motivation, overruling all other considerations and/or attracting those to the job who are motivated by it exclusively and not by caring motivations. Instead of their working more willingly and better, the labor supply is likely to be reduced and the activity undertaken less intensively.

Yet empirical observations of changes in behavior and policy proposals are different and should not be mixed. Even if studies have shown the crowding-out of intrinsic motivation under certain specific circumstances, the conclusion that non-payment should be a precondition for preserving the quality of caring services would run the danger of neglecting a fundamentally important issue, namely, that material resources are needed to sustain both care giver and care receiver in the caring relationship. Alienation need not be linked to remuneration, and caring motivation in a care giver does not necessarily become less caring once it is outfitted with the material scope for providing adequate care on the basis of an income.[31] The conditions under which a crowding-out of caring motivation may take place must be carefully studied. Low wages for care givers might be one of the reasons. (Nelson 1998)[32] Caution, therefore, is needed, and appropriate distinctions should be made in any transfer of the observations and conclusions of Crowding-out Theory.

Summary

The observations of Crowding Theory are of interest in the study of the social organization of caring activities, yet two aspects should be kept in mind:

(1) The first relates to the empirical situation. The central hypothesis of Crowding Theory is that the presence of intrinsic motivation increases the susceptibility to crowding-out. According to this, caring situations would be expected to be extremely sensitive to crowding-out. But not all intrinsic motivations are caring – and not every intrinsic motivation may be prone to crowding-out. One has to be careful in transferring the observations of Crowding Theory to caring situations too quickly. There are several reasons for this. The empirical situations in which the crowding-out of intrinsic motivation has been observed have not been typical caring situations. And even more important: they have not been dependency situations. Furthermore, caring activities do not appear among the intrinsically motivated activities that are prone to crowding-out as conceptualized by Crowding Theory. The provision of caring activities and the performance of dependency services could well react quite differently. With regard to caring motivations, therefore, the question of whether (all) caring motivations can be crowded-out (at least within a single individual) must remain open for future research.

(2) The second aspect to remember concerns the policy conclusions from the empirical relationship between extrinsic and intrinsic motivation. Paying too much attention to the motivational aspect of caring not only enhances the danger of emotionalizing and privatizing it. It also tends to transfer

---

[31] Folbre and Nelson argue that markets for caring services are often examples of "'rich' markets in which the movement of money is only one dimension in a complex relationship [of the participants involved] including elements of (when it is going well) trust, affection, and appreciation" (Folbre and Nelson 2000: 130-131). See also Nelson 1999.

[32] See also Chapter 7 on the possible crowding-out effect of material dependency.

crowding-out arguments in their crude version and fosters the conclusion that, in order to preserve intrinsic caring motivations, caring work best not be paid – as expressed in Folbre's "paradox of caring labor." In caring situations, the question of the material basis for these activities has a significance which must be carefully considered. (see Chapters 6 and 7)

Thus, one would have to strongly question the notion that caring activities should not be paid if their distinct quality is to be preserved. In drawing conclusions for caring, caution and careful differentiation must be observed. Still, two-fold concepts could benefit from a more differentiated application of the insights of Crowding Theory – in terms both of possible crowding-out and possible crowding-in. This topic and, more specifically, the encouragement of intrinsic motivation through policy measures will be taken up in Chapter 8.

Caring as a constitutive act

The discussion of the applicability of Crowding Theory, however, brings an aspect to the fore which takes up the issues and impact of caring motivations from a different perspective, yet feeds back into a theme recurrent throughout the previous chapters, namely, the assumption of choice behavior with regard to the provision of caring services.

The distinction between motivation and activity as elaborated by two-fold concepts of caring is one possible perspective from which to analyze phenomena. However, analysis has shown that motivations involving welfare calculations appear – at least in their analytical form – to be options of personal choice. As Susan Himmelweit (1996) points out, the dualistic treatment of motivation versus activity risks putting too much emphasis on choice behavior: individuals would seem to be able to choose the degree to which the welfare of others interferes with, enhances, or disadvantages their own personal welfare. But as was pointed out in Chapter 2, caring – especially the performance of caring services for dependents – is not always a purposive activity in the sense that people may choose to perform this activity or not. Especially with regard to the existential dependency of the care receiver on the care giver in dependency situations "not caring is not usually an operational alternative" (Himmelweit 1996: 9). Not caring is not conceived as an option since caring itself structures people's lives, and the lives of many care receivers hinge on their care givers. Individuals "find themselves caring not because they consciously choose to do so but because of social norms that both legitimate the needs of certain people [e.g. children] and give them a call on the time and energy of others in particular relationships to them." (Himmelweit 1999: 29) As long, however, as care givers would seem to be able to choose freely, this offers a specific perspective for assessing the kinds of relation which exist between care givers and care receivers.[33]

Caring behavior may also reflect a sense of identity involving the recognition of other persons' goals and the mutual interdependencies involved and must ultimately also be considered a social matter. (Sen 1987: 85) In this sense, the performance of dependency services inspired by values central to a person's character and identity as well as other intrinsic motivations is not so much the result of choice behavior. Rather, it may be understood as a *constitutive act*, connected to the identity of the care giver and created and developed by her/his relationship with the care receiver. The performance of the caring activity is not separated from life and self but constitutive of the dependency workers and not separate from their relations with other people. (Radin 1996: 105)[34] As Julie Nelson has stressed, responsibility, for example, has more to do with *who one is*, and less with *what one does*. (Nelson 1998) In cases where caring is a constitutive act, no crowding-out would be possible, since the motivation for caring would be rooted in an individual's identity and not under the individual's control.[35]

The concept of identity – an individual's image of his or her personal identity and of the identity of others – is central to integrative caring relationships.[36] At the core of a caring relationship lies a statement such as "'I will do something or I will ask you to do something because of what I am and because of what you are'. What I am is what I think I am. What you are in the above statement is what I think you are. It may not be the same as what you think you are, but it is still the image of identity to which the appeal is made" (Boulding 1978: 190). The structure of perceived identities in the case of caring leads into corresponding patterns of benevolence – not indifference – generating one-way transfers. Care givers in these cases will remain in caring situations because their morals, their feelings of right and wrong, their identity as humans would be violated if they left. They have no choice of exit since doing so would go against their very identities.[37]

The concept of identity does not include utility calculations or a conception of choice between two utilities. The concept of identity in this

---

[33] In theories about the state of present-day societies there is doubtless a widespread pessimism that the degree of connectedness may very well decrease over historic time.

[34] Cf. the concept of caring work in this chapter.

[35] Sevenhuijsen questions the importance ascribed to issues of identity as opposed to acting or doing. (e.g. Sevenhuijsen 1998)

[36] According to Boulding, the image of one's identity is a complex structure made up by one's bodily self-image and one's own knowledge, memories, skills, and potentialities, as well as the roles one assumes in social structures and institutions. (Boulding 1978: 190)

[37] These reasons for staying differ from other possible reasons of care givers to remain in a caring situation such as the fear that the situation will deteriorate for the care receiver in their absence or because the "products" of caring are public goods from whose consumption there is no escape. On the difficulty to exit from public goods see Hirschman 1970: 98.

sense is fundamentally different from the concept of choice. To avoid the creation of yet another dualism between choice behavior and constitutive acts, Nelson proposes a "conceptual middle ground of [...] 'influenced choices' or 'roles with some freedom'" (Nelson 1998: 15) which would reflect "*both* the agent's constitution in connection with his or her social and natural environment and his or her individual behavior" (Nelson 1998; see also Nelson 1996: 31-33). According to Nelson, the notion of responsibility is central to theorizing the provisioning of caring and dependency situations, and policies which aim at encouraging more caring behavior have to complement motivational aspects of "rewards" and "incentives" by considerations of the identities of the persons involved and vice versa. (Nelson 1998)

As all identities, however, care givers' identities are also socially and culturally constructed. (e.g. Nussbaum 1999: 253-261) They still, for example, reflect an underlying gender division of labor. (Abel and Nelson 1990) Accordingly, one must always ask which of society's members have identities constructed as care giving identities and which members of society are prohibited from exiting caring situations.

The issues of caring motivations, of the importance of the moral dimension in caring, of identity and choice, are of crucial importance when studying caring situations and will be taken up further on in this study.

The conceptual approaches to caring in economics discussed in Part II conceptualized important aspects of caring activities. But they also neglected crucial ones. It became clear that caring has a (strong) motivation component – a fact stressed by two-fold caring concepts and also acknowledged by New Home Economics. Yet, it is obvious that reliance on caring motivations alone involves risks for the care receiver. Two-fold concepts of caring not only elaborate the specific features of caring motivations but also point out that caring has a strong work component. By focusing on the motivation and activity involved in caring, however, most concepts tend to neglect the resources needed to sustain effective caring relationships – despite their importance in the debate on adequate pay for caring services.

III

TOWARD AN INTEGRATED ANALYSIS OF CARING

Part III will address the open questions identified in the analysis in Part II. To treat the unresolved issues uncovered by the discussion thus far and contribute to an economic analysis of caring, two additional ingredients are required: a) a conceptual framework to integrate the various theoretical approaches and, associated with it, b) a more detailed understanding of the asymmetries and dependencies involved in the provision of caring services.

As a first step a *component concept* of an effective caring situation will be developed to serve as the analytic framework. The second step will be to systematize asymmetries and dependencies for use as central categories of analysis for caring situations. As a third step the two will be brought together as constituent parts in the systematic application of a theoretical basis for analyzing caring activities and evaluating caring policies.

Chapter 6

CARING CONCEPTUALIZED AS THE RESULT OF AN EFFECTIVE CARING SITUATION

The three components constituting an effective caring situation

The component concept of an effective caring situation relies on the main assumption that it is possible to identify certain characteristic analytical features common to all types of caring activities and treat them within a single frame of reference. The activities comprise caring for the self, caring among equals, and caring for dependents; the caring may be paid or unpaid, performed in the domestic sphere, in a civic context, in a market or state-welfare system, by women or men, or in the formal or the informal economy. The concept of a *caring situation* proposed in the following is an analytical construct that conceptualizes the (idealtype) situation in which an effective caring activity is provided. It may be used as a frame of reference for the study and as a tool in analyzing the provision of caring activities of any type.

Figure 1: The caring situation

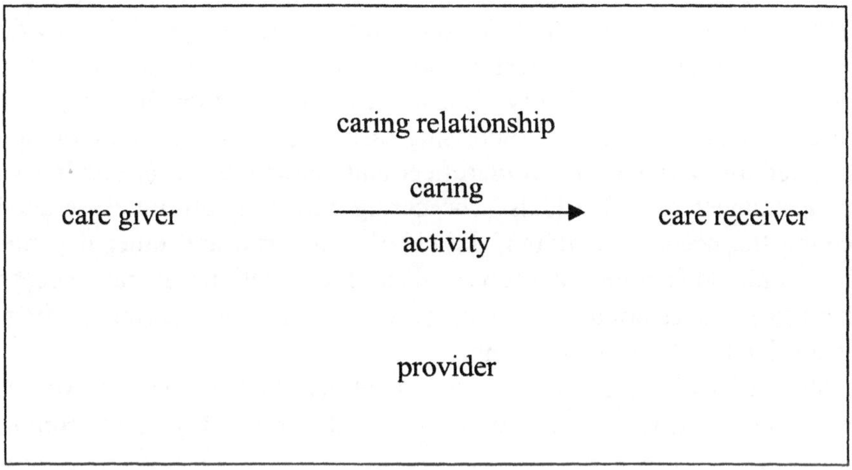

The concept of a *caring situation* assumes the effective performance of a caring activity[1] characterized by the presence of a specific unilocational

[1] It thus presupposes the integral completion of all four phases of the caring process as discussed by Tronto 1993: 105-108. See Chapter 2, Note 5.

caring relationship between a *care giver* and a *care receiver*. The care giver is the person performing the caring activity, doing the hands-on caring work at the location of the care receiver. The care receiver is the person toward whose needs the caring activity is directed and who benefits from the performance of the activity. Care giver and care receiver together constitute the direct caring relationship. The caring relationship must be sustained by resources coming from the *provider* of the relationship. The resources may come from within the caring relationship if the care giver or the care receiver provides them. They may also come from a provider or providing institution outside the caring relationship.[2]

A caring situation is composed of three analytically separate conceptual components: a *motivation component*, a *work component* and a *resource component*. *Together* they permit the effective performance of a caring activity. The following presentation of the three components is based on the analysis in Part II of this study. It systematizes the findings above and addresses the critical points.

(1) Initiating and continuing a caring situation: the motivation component

The motivation component is an expression of the fact that a benevolent caring motivation is essential for a successful caring situation. Any caring motivation must include a benevolent awareness of the situation of the other and her/his well-being, reflecting both individuals' *need for care* and their *responsibility to care*. Caring motivations reflect the relatedness, the attachment of the caring protagonist to other individuals: they bring into perspective and focus on the situation of the care receiver and thereby differ from the unattached self-interest commonly assumed for the autonomous individual in economic theory. Self-interest alone cannot fully explain the entire spectrum of attitudes comprising caring behavior. Rather, motivations identified as *caring motivations* reflect and confirm the connectedness and the relatedness of individuals. The caring motive is absolutely crucial to meeting the needs of children, the elderly, the sick, and other dependents who cannot look after themselves; these are situations of bare necessity, where caring does not amount to social choice. However, caring motives are not confined to this type of caring.

Motivations behind caring activities are manifold. As was shown above, they may be divided into two main categories. The first comprises

[2] Conceptualizing a caring situation in such a way includes, of course, analytical simplification in the sense that a single care giver might, in reality, have to attend to more than one care receiver (as is the case, for example, in families and nursing homes) and/or one care receiver might have more than one care giver to look after him/her. There might also be different providers sustaining a single caring relationship (as is the case where family income and state subsidies go together in the provision of child care).

motivations that are inspired by some kind of welfare or utility considerations that concern and involve the assessment and satisfaction of needs and yet extend beyond unattached self-interest (specific altruism, long-term expectations of reciprocity, commitment). In the second category are motivations that are not based on utility and welfare considerations; rather, they originate from moral considerations[3] arising out of social relationships (responsibility and obligation), or from other intrinsic motivations (emotion and affection).

The hypothesis here is that only caring motivations that generate the integrative product bring about effective caring situations. In this respect, the caring motivation may be considered as part of the competence of the persons involved in a caring situation. And at a general level, it not only relates to the care giver but includes the provider (and the care receiver) as well. There are many situations where an instrumental caring service is performed but no integrative product is created since they are the product of motivations unrelated to caring.

The degree to which expectations of a return from the care receiver matter is crucial for caring motivations. Caring motivations take the situation of the care receiver as the starting point to determine what must be done. And in extreme caring cases, they must also make possible caring situations where no return is to be expected from the care receiver. The decisive point is the care receiver's needs (on which her/his very survival may depend).

(2) Establishing and maintaining a caring relationship: the work component

But motivation alone is not enough. The care receiver can be helped only if a hands-on caring activity is performed by the care giver [G] for the benefit of the care receiver [R]. And the work component embodies this fact.

Performing an effective caring activity as well as providing an effective caring service also requires caring skills – some of them codifiable in terms of a formal training scheme, others tacit and acquired in the course of caring for a particular care receiver. (e.g. Himmelweit 1999: 34) Caring skills include the care giver's ability to perform instrumental aspects of the caring service such as the know-how involved in helping the elderly and infirm out of bed and competence in communicative aspects. This latter aspect presupposes a caring disposition for such work, an ability to handle the complex situations of need evaluation, and communication skills. Caring

---

[3] As was discussed above, the distinction between (1) and (2) is important with regard to caring; also, altruistically motivated caring is not synonymous with morally motivated caring.

skills are not "just natural;" nor can "just natural" skills, much less no skills, suffice.[4]

By the performance of a caring activity [G ->] a direct caring relationship [G -> R] is established between care giver and care receiver; this is especially evident in cases of other-care but also holds for cases of self-care, where care giver and care receiver are identical.

(3) Providing for and sustaining a caring relationship: the resource component

The resource component is an expression of the fact that caring relationships are not self-contained. Their success or failure hinges not only on the good will and skill of the care giver and the care receiver but also depends on a variety of resources that can be analytically separated from the work component.

The resource component is comprised of the material and/or financial flow needed to sustain a caring relationship and the time allotted to provide an individual caring service. If it is to function, the caring relationship between care giver and care receiver must be materially and/or financially sustained at least over a lengthy period of time. Two important aspects of the material and/or financial provision must be distinguished: on the one hand, the care giver needs the material and/or financial resources to respond appropriately to the care receiver's needs. On the other hand, the care giver her/himself must be sustained or will otherwise be unable to perform the caring service. Account must be taken of both the perspective of the care receiver as well as that of the care giver. (This argument takes on special importance, for example, in the discussion of financial compensation for care givers.)

A second important resource for the provision of an effective caring activity is time. Caring activities are time-intensive in two respects. First, performance of a single caring activity requires an amount of time that usually exceeds the time allotted for purely instrumental aspects of the work (e.g. the time needed to bathe a person) since there must also be time for the communicative aspects of caring activities (e.g. talking and listening to the care receiver) and for arriving at and returning from the caring location. Second, in cases such as child or elderly care, the caring relationship must also continue through time for the caring activities to be fully effective and achieve their goal.

As shall be discussed in more detail in Chapter 7, the resource component may be socially organized inside or outside the direct caring

---

4 A fact which is gaining in importance in view of changes in the social structure such as increased life expectancy, growing needs in an aging society, and new (professional) standards for health and treatment.

relationship. Where the resource component is organized outside the relationship, neither the care giver nor the care receiver provide the material and/or financial resources (or have an influence on the time allocated for performance of the caring activity); rather, these resources are provided or controlled by an additional person, a group of persons, or an institution – the *provider(s)* [P]. The provider(s) may be responsible for the availability of only *some* of the external resources and, in some cases, may not actually *provide* resources but merely *control* their flow to and within the (household) caring relationship.

The introduction of the role of the resource provider alongside to the caring relationship between care giver and care receiver renders the conceptual construct of a caring situation more complex. If the resources needed by the caring relationship are integrated into the model rather than regarded as a given constant, then the source of material support and possibly of time control, namely, another person or an institution may enter the equation. The component concept of a caring situation, therefore, allows for bilateral situations if the provider comes from within the caring relationship, as well as for multilateral situations if the provider comes from outside the caring relationship.

An integrated perspective

The main hypothesis of this study is that it is the very combination of the components motivation, work, and resources that characterizes the effective performance of caring activities understood as the satisfaction and fulfillment of caring needs. The interaction of all three components determines the quality, extent, and kind of the caring activity performed. Consequently, all three components must be present and functional if an effective caring situation is to be brought into being and continued.

Although the three components of effective performance of caring activities can be analytically separated and conceptualized, they should be studied and analyzed from an integrated perspective. All three have to be taken into account when studying caring since it is only *together* that they constitute a caring situation and ensure the effective performance of a caring activity. Work and motivation alone, without resources, cannot sustain a caring relationship and provide for a dependency situation over time. The resource component is useless in the absence of a motivated and capable care giver. And as important as motivation may be in initiating the performance of a caring activity, it can neither perform the work nor sustain a caring relationship. Even in the case of strong caring motivation, the self-sacrificing care giver must be able to perform the caring activity and to secure the resources to sustain both the person cared for and her/himself. Undue emphasis of the role of a single component in bringing a caring situation about, and neglect of the importance of the others, may thus result in a distorted analysis of caring situations. The conceptualization of and analysis of caring built upon the three components outlined above avoids this danger by stressing the importance of all three components.

By including the role of the provider alongside the caring relationship, the component concept of a caring situation allows for the view of caring situations as multilateral situations. Within the concept of a caring situation, the perspectives of those involved in the caring relationship – care giver and care receiver – may be studied. But the analysis can additionally be extended to include the perspective of the material and/or financial provider and the institutions outside the caring relationship. The concept of a caring situation thus enables the study of all the economic actors involved in the provision of a caring service. Unlike concepts that focus either on the care receiver or the care giver and usually confine themselves to a single perspective, the concept of a caring situation draws attention to the three components, makes possible the study of effective caring from all these different perspectives, and still furnishes a common frame of reference. The perspective focuses on the situation of the care giver as well as that of the care receiver, and on the respective asymmetries and dependencies affecting them. By broadening the analyzing perspective to include not only the relationship between the care giver and the care receiver but also the interactions with the resource provider, various caring situations in different realms of the economy may be considered. As shall be discussed below, this characteristic of the concept is especially relevant for studying questions of economic justice.

Basic structures of caring situations

As indicated by the component concept, the caring relationship between care giver and care receiver [G → R] must be materially (financially) sustained if a caring service is to be secured. In analytical terms, the resource component may be socially organized in a number of different ways vis-à-vis the caring relationship, thus producing a variety of caring situation structures. All of them are analytical. Different combinations are possible and exist. Not all of them constitute asymmetric caring situations, nor do they necessarily feature material dependency.

The analytical possibilities of organizing the resource component vis-à-vis the caring relationship fall into three broader groups.[5] (1) The resource

[5] For analytical purposes the cases are based on three restrictions: First, only labor grants are considered to constitute a caring relationship, whereas labor grant G → is different from money grant P →. Second, the resource component P must be directed explicitly toward

component may be located within the caring relationship itself. (2) The resource component may be located outside the caring relationship. (3) The resource component may be located partly inside and partly outside the caring relationship.

(1) Location of the resource component within the caring relationship

The resource component may be located within the caring relationship itself. In personal terms, the work component and the resource component would in this case not be strictly separate. Three sub cases may be distinguished here: (a) the care giver sustains the caring relationship as in the case of an income-earning single parent; (b) the care receiver sustains the caring relationship as in informal cases such as an adult son/daughter giving care to sick or frail elderly parents as well as in formal cases such as a paid care giver who is hired by the dependent sick, disabled, or elderly person by her/himself; (c) care giver and care receiver together materially sustain the caring relationship. In this case, giver and receiver have separate sources of income and the caring service is performed as a strict one-way transfer, as in volunteer help provided by a neighbor to assist an elderly person in dressing, or help in minding the children. In each of these three cases (a) – (c) the caring situation is *bilateral.*

(2) Location of the resource component outside the caring relationship

The resource component may also be located outside the caring relationship. Here, the work and resource components are, in personal terms, strictly separate. The caring relationship is sustained by one or more providers (person(s) or institution(s)) personally distinct from the care giver/care receiver. In this case the provider does not enter the direct caring relationship but adds to the number of people participating and creates a *multilateral* caring situation.

Two basic sub cases may be distinguished here. In the first sub case, a provider who is personally distinct from care giver and care receiver sustains the entire relationship. Care giver and care receiver both rely on the same provider. Examples include family situations where full-time income earning and full-time care giving are divided between spouses or partners (bread-winner/care-giver families) in the informal realm, and institutional

---

sustaining the caring relationship, that is, if a volunteer worker is supported by his/her spouse, P will be considered located with G and not as a resource received from outside (since the spouse does not explicitly support G to do volunteer work toward R). Third, although a single care giver may have to care for several dependents or a single dependent may rely on several care givers, and the outside providers may be numerous as well, each of their respective involvements in the dependency situation is depicted separately, that is, for analytical purposes, G, R, and P are assumed to be single persons/ entities.

arrangements in the formal realm such as a care giver hired to care for a dependent care receiver by a family member who also materially supports the care receiver. In the second sub case, the caring relationship is sustained by two separate providers; care giver and care receiver rely on different providers. An example is a situation where the state finances a social care worker for an elderly person who is otherwise supported by the family.

(3) Location of the resource component partly inside and partly outside the caring relationship

A third possibility of organizing the resource component in a caring situation is the mixed case where the resource component is partly located inside and partly outside the caring relationship. Either (a) the care giver gets material support from outside the caring relationship, as in cases of a care giver hired by a person outside the caring relationship, the latter who is not additionally supporting the care receiver, or adult children hiring and paying a care giver for an elderly parent but not supporting the parent, or (b) the care receiver gets material support from an outside provider such as in child support from a divorced parent, or a sick parent who still supports his/her caring children gets sick money from the state.

The control over both time and material resources may be situated with the same person or institution, as in the case of nursing homes, where the employer of the care giver – apart from managing the material and financial flow of resources – is also able to control the time allocated to care giving tasks. But time and resource control may also be divided. As shall be shown in Chapters 7 and 8, the location of the resource component with regard to the caring relationship also has consequences for the market demand for caring services.

The analysis of caring institutions

The component concept itself is pre-institutional. It reflects the core elements of the caring situation as such, that is, *before* this situation is further shaped or transformed by informal or formal institutional arrangements – whether caring activities are paid or unpaid, provided within the family, by the market, by the state, or within the networks of civil society. It conceptualizes the provision of different caring activities irrespective of the particular economic sphere in which their performance occurs. Its conceptual insights, therefore, are not restricted to any one specific economic sphere (e.g. the household).

And yet, the component concept of a caring situation paves the way for the study of institutional questions. Precisely because of its pre-institutional character the component concept can serve as a frame of reference for the study of the social and economic organization of caring activities in two important respects: it provides a helpful framework to understand and evaluate the social and economic organization of caring situations in general and, more particularly, the specific institutional arrangements in the provision of caring.

At a general level, any social and economic organization of caring services must match caring services with caring needs. And it must ensure the effective combination of the motivation, work, and resource components of caring situations. Different coordination mechanisms and their manner of operation in different realms of the economy result in different combinations of the three components and affect both the characteristics and the structure of their respective interrelationship. (see Chapter 7)

The different combinations of the three components manifest themselves in different formal or informal institutional arrangements in which the caring services are provided (e.g. family, state nursing home, or mobile caring service). The respective structures of these institutions thus reflect a given combination of the motivation, work, and resource components, manifesting a specific form of social and economic organization of caring activities.

The basic structures of caring situations which may underlie any single institutional arrangements provide helpful tools for the analysis of these arrangements. Since the ways in which the three components may be institutionalized (i.e. socially and economically organized) differ in the way they deal with the actual and potential asymmetries and dependencies inherent in caring situations, the basic structures offer insights into the asymmetries and dependencies arising from given institutional arrangements.

A significant feature of any institution, whether it be family structures, a commercial nursing home, a government program, or neighborhood help system, is thus the manner and combination in which these various institutional arrangements for caring services bring together the work, resources, and motivation components. And more specifically, how in doing so these institutional arrangements address the main features of a given caring situation, that is, how the specific institutional arrangement deals with the asymmetries involved. Does it enhance them? Does it alleviate or aggravate the existential, material, and motivational dependencies involved? The different types of actual or potential asymmetries and dependencies involved in the provision of caring services therefore deserve special analysis.

Chapter 7

ASYMMETRIES AND DEPENDENCIES IN CARING SITUATIONS AS CENTRAL CATEGORIES OF ANALYSIS

In the analysis of caring situations, the asymmetries and dependencies involved deserve special attention. Different types of asymmetries and dependencies will therefore be systematized and analyzed in greater detail in this chapter.

Whereas the component concept provides the analytic framework, the analysis of caring situations would remain incomplete without a more detailed and systematic understanding of actual and potential asymmetries and dependencies involved in the provision of caring services. Such an understanding is of interest all the more so since, as the following analysis will show, their impact within the framework of an analysis of caring extends beyond their importance as characteristics of caring situations. Rather, this study regards asymmetries and dependencies as the central categories for analyzing caring situations. If used in this valuable analytical role, they not only provide additional keys to the understanding of caring, but also enable an analysis which can bring together the disparate findings of existing approaches to caring in economics, thereby facilitating an integrated perspective.

Just as the work, resource, and motivation components, the respective asymmetries and dependencies connected to them also come together in various combinations in caring situations. The component concept helps to specify and localize them. The following analysis is meant to distinguish analytical possibilities that, although sometimes appearing extreme, provide useful tools for the examining concrete institutions and institutional arrangements in caring situations. The analytical differentiation of the work, resource, and motivation components may also serve to highlight the three different types of asymmetries and dependency: asymmetry in capabilities and existential dependency belong to the work component; asymmetry in resource control and material dependency are part of the resource component; and caring motivations and motivational exit barriers are found within the motivation component. The various asymmetries and dependencies, in turn, shed light on the way the three components relate to one another.

Asymmetry in capabilities and existential dependency

Caring situations feature qualitatively and quantitatively asymmetric relations marked by differences in the starting positions of the partners involved.[1] At the core of a dependency caring situation is the existential need of the care receiver and his/her inability to meet this need by his/her own performance of the relevant dependency service. The asymmetry in capabilities between care receiver and care giver and the care receiver's resulting existential dependency on the effective performance of a caring activity constitute the beginning of the analysis. More specifically, asymmetries in capabilities have a decisive influence on the autonomy of the care receiver. This influence may manifest itself in different ways as will be explained in the following.

The incapability of meeting existential needs on one's own

The care receiver's limited ability or even incapability to perform own-account caring services in a dependency caring situation is the source of the asymmetry in capabilities between care receiver and care giver. The fact that the need in question relates to life sustainment aggravates this circumstance. Taken together this has a decisive impact on the dependent's overall choice with regard to the entry into as well as the exit from a caring situation.

The need for caring services is existential for a dependent care receiver, i.e. the care receiver's very life requires the performance of the caring service by a person other than her/himself. Waiving the service is therefore not a viable alternative for dependent care receivers. Their need for caring services is thus inelastic.[2] In other words, the existentially dependent care receiver has no choice but to enter into a caring situation nor is there a choice to exit.[3]

---

1 Cf. also Biesecker 1996.

2 A certain individual as well as societal need for caring activities (though possibly varying in degree) is constant (because of the inevitability of these needs as discussed in Chapter 2); it arises and must be responded to, whether this need and the accompanying preferences are revealed on the market or not. People need dependency services even without market demand for these services, be it because dependent care receivers cannot afford to buy them or be it the needed services are not (yet?) supplied by the market. The possibility of voicing the need for caring services in the market, exercising market demand, is the privilege of those who have the financial means to do so. Market demand for dependency services in this sense is merely an indicator for a group of (privileged) members of society who can afford to demand dependency services via the market and not for the need of these services in general.

3 The existentiality of needs together with their inelasticity create emergency situations in which it is especially apparent that someone else has to take the care receiver's needs as a starting point for action. People most often feel the need to help in these situations.

The inability to self-satisfy existential needs may extend across a wide spectrum. A robust but mentally confused elderly person may have the physical capability for self-care but lacks the mental capacity to do so. Fully paralyzed but mentally aware patients and frail but mentally aware elderly persons conversely lack the physical capabilities for self-care. Of course, there are also combinations of the two, as in the case of infants or persons with multiple mental and physical disabilities. It is important to study closely care receivers' type of incapability because of its decisive influence on their ability to decide themselves on specific care givers or specific caring services.

Outside identification of needs and determination of preferences

In a dependency situation, the limited autonomy of the care receiver, whether temporary or permanent, may involve the inability to express and specify the caring service needed. This may be due to the age or to the mental and physical health of the care receiver. Young children, the severely ill, mentally confused or handicapped elderly, and disabled individuals are hardly in a position to name and specify the kind of dependency services that must be performed by the care giver. In these cases of extreme dependency, some person *other* than the care receiver has to identify the dependent's needs, take them as the starting point for action and determinate how to satisfy them. But this is not the case for all caring situations for dependents and varies according to the care receiver's degree of mental autonomy. Unlike a small child, for example, an elderly person who relies on a dependency worker, although bodily frail, might still be in a mental state allowing him/her to precisely voice and identify the specific dependency services needed.

In some caring situations, the outside identification of needs for care receivers who are autonomous in terms of their mental capabilities may also result from a certain structural intransparency of needs.[4] Such situations in which the needs of care receivers have to be identified by outside persons are apparent in areas such as health care. Here, dependent care receivers would be able to articulate the dependency services needed but, due to their lack of medical knowledge, they are confronted by structural intransparency (the patient, in principle, does not know what is good for him/her) and therefore require the outside determination of needs and demands. An outside person, frequently the care giver as producer of the service, determines demand. (e.g. Herder-Dorneich 1980: 151)

One clearly visible problem immediately concerns the issue of who is to identify the – objective and subjective – needs, and eventually, how best to

[4] Note similarities to other consultancy situations producing credence goods or experience goods. See e.g. Ottnad 2000a: 475.

meet them. "What must be done," however, is by no means always easy to determine. It entails intensive discourse on needs, which involves "social interpretations and conflicting notions of what constitutes good care" (Sevenhuijsen 1998: 20). Who determines best the specific caring need in a given caring situation? The care giver, care receiver, a third party such as a doctor, health inspector, politician – or the taxpayer? Perceptions of need can naturally err. There may also be confusion as to whose needs are to be the object of care and how the specific needs in question can be identified and satisfied. As in other economic situations, a problem of ignorance may arise. The manner in which care givers choose to meet established or defined needs can present additional problems. Different perceptions of need and appropriate responses may conflict deeply, just as may the needs of the care receiver and the care giver in given situations. In such cases, the main issues to be addressed concern the ways and means by which the distribution of caring services is to be assured and the right coordinating mechanism to best direct their performance – matters that address the social organization of caring.

Outside control of resources

The mental and physical condition of the care receiver may also inhibit her/his control over resources – even if they are the care receiver's own resources. A dependent care receiver may, therefore, also experience the outside control of resources either by the care giver or an outside provider. Only where care receivers control their own resources can they determine their demand for dependency services on the market.

Existential dependency

The care receiver's limited autonomy, his/her incapability for self-care, together with the existential nature of the caring need, make up existential dependency. The asymmetry of capabilities creates an *existential dependency* on the part of the care receiver with regard to the performance of a caring service by a care giver. In some extreme though not uncommon cases, the existential dependency of the care receiver on the performance of the needed caring service may manifest itself as an existential dependency on a particular care giver. If there is only one possible care giver at hand, the care receiver has to rely on that particular person to perform the caring service required. In such a case, the care giver has a performance monopoly vis-à-vis the care receiver. There is no choice but to accept the services regardless of the quality level. The care receiver enjoys no choice of entry into or exit from the caring relationship and is existentially dependent on what the dependency worker does or refrains from doing. The cost of exit for the care receiver is high – it can range from loss of lifelong personal ties to loss of life, with such intermediate stages as deprivation of livelihood.

Cases of care receivers' existential dependency on particular care givers are extreme.[5] And such a pattern of *care monopolies*, as these situations may be described, are not uncommon. In fact, many care givers hold monopolies over the care receivers they attend to as, for example, parents over their children, adult children over their frail elderly parents if they care for them at home, and nursing homes over the elderly in their charge. It could also be argued that even in non-monopoly type situations of provision where the care giver has a choice among several care givers, the single care giver holds the power of capabilities (an existential power) in the actual performance of the caring service, and therefore a quasi-monopoly. (Abel and Nelson 1990a: 25)

This circumstance also sheds light on the importance and limits of choice in caring situations: above all in situations of existential dependency, where there is no choice with regard to the general performance of a caring service, the choice as to who will perform it (and exercise existential power over the care receiver) becomes all the more important. The choice is theoretically broadened with caring services for dependents provided via the market or by civil society where the recipient may theoretically choose from a greater number of helpers. But in practice, a polipolistic structure exists here as well. (Abel and Nelson 1990a, Plantenga and Bettio 1998)

Asymmetry in resource control and material dependency

The analytical structures of caring situations as described in Chapter 6 represent different organizational arrangements of the work and resource components. It is helpful for the analysis of caring situations to analytically distinguish these structural cases in the study of the social organization of caring situations and gain insights on possible material asymmetries and dependencies since the different possibilities of organizing the resource component in a caring situation have an effect on possible material asymmetries and dependencies. They may include asymmetries in material resource control among care receiver, care giver, and provider which may lead to different forms of informal or formal material (economic) dependency of the entire caring relationship, the care receiver, and the care giver.

---

[5] These situations are very frequent with regard to classic caring situations although not considered common in economics, since "in economic interactions it is rarely that case that one player is at the complete mercy of another player" (Fehr and Schmidt 2000).

The structure of any given caring situation has an influence on the asymmetries and dependencies involved. Different institutional arrangements can be evaluated in terms of the effect their caring situation structure has on asymmetries and dependencies. The material asymmetry of care giver and care receiver with regard to the provider is induced and enhanced if dependency situations are organized in such a way that the resource component is personally separate from the caring relationship, i.e. if the work and resource components are provided by different persons. A functional separation of the two components, i.e. the organization of the resource component outside the direct caring relationship through an outside provider, might act to enhance material dependency. In this case, the direct influence of the care giver – as that of the care receiver – on the quality and extent as well as the shaping of the work component diminishes, since the caring relationship itself is dependent on other persons or institutions for support. The asymmetry in material resource control between the dependency relationship partners and an outside provider enhances the possibility of material dependency of care giver and receiver. It weakens their bargaining power and limits their options of voice and exit.

With *material dependency*, the care receiver or care giver may be unable to exit a caring situation as the result of their limited control over resources. Material dependency is economic dependency. Access to and control over resources is an economic (bargaining) power (strictly understood). And the person or institution controlling the resources has a quite powerful economic position. The location of the resource component, and the material dependencies it may imply, can have a decisive influence in shaping the work component by facilitating or preventing the choice of alternative care givers to attend to the care receiver. Material dependency not only affects the care receiver. It may involve the care giver as well. The respective situations of both persons must be taken into account to fully understand the complex structures behind the providing of caring services.[6]

Not all the analytical cases presented above involve materially asymmetric caring situations, nor do they necessarily entail material dependency. In cases where care giver and care receiver support the caring relationship, for example, there is no material asymmetry between the persons involved. In cases where there is an asymmetry in the access to and

[6] Under certain institutional conditions, material dependency can become "exploitable dependency." Exploitable dependency in economic terms is understood as an asymmetrical relationship which is characterized not only by the fact that the recipient needs the service or resource which the worker or material provider supplies in the sense that the recipient cannot supply the resource, the good, or the service by her/himself, but also that the recipient depends on a *particular* worker or material provider for the services or resources, and the worker or material provider enjoys discretionary control over the service or resource that the recipient needs. (Fraser 1997: 46)

control of resources, however, the result may be a material dependency of the care receiver on the care giver, or on a provider of resources from outside the caring relationship, as well as the material dependency of the care giver on the care receiver, or on the outside provider. Whereas the asymmetry in capabilities discussed above appears as an asymmetry within the work component, asymmetry in resource endowment appears as an asymmetry involving both the work and the resource component.

It is possible to formulate some fundamental hypotheses on the impact of the respective structure of a caring situation (the location of the resource component in relation to the work component) on the likeliness of material dependency. These will now be outlined.

Material asymmetry within the caring relationship

If the resource component is located inside the caring relationship, either care giver or care receiver or both control the resource flow. With asymmetry in resource control between the two, the care giver may be materially dependent on the care receiver. In this case, the care receiver may face existential dependency but not material dependency. The care receiver, at least materially, can leave the caring situation – provided that there are alternative sources of care giving which can be accessed by money. If, on the other hand, the care receiver must materially rely on the care giver, in addition to the care receiver's existential dependency on that person (as in cases of parents caring for their children or adult children caring for their parents), the power of capabilities and skills which the care giver holds over the care receiver is further enhanced and the care receiver's vulnerability vis-à-vis that particular person increases. Since, however, caring motivation is assumed in the care giver, the danger of an abuse of this power is lessened. Of course, the care giver might also be materially dependent on the care receiver in cases where the elderly parent is sustaining the caring relationship with an adult child. The existential dependency of the care receiver then meets (and counterbalances?) the material dependency of the care giver.

Material asymmetry between the caring relationship and an outside provider

A strict separation of the work and resource components results in the asymmetry of resource endowment between the partners in the caring relationship on the one side and the outside provider of the resources on the other. If care giver and care receiver rely on the same provider, the caring relationship depends on a single outside provider for material support. The provider in this case has a monopoly over material provision and the control of resources. Although there is no asymmetry in resource endowment between care giver and care receiver, there is an asymmetry distinguishing them from their common provider. Care giver as well as care receiver can thus be materially dependent on the provider.

If care giver and care receiver are supported separately and rely on different providers, the caring relationship is supported by two providers. Sole control by a single outside provider is lessened, and the material power divided. Although the existential dependency of the care receiver remains, the possibility of material dependency is lessened. Material dependency on a single provider does not now arise. If one of the providers stops providing, the caring relationship could possibly be continued for at least some time with the help of the second provider.

The functional separation of the resource and work components, that is, the organization of the resource component outside the direct caring relationship, may thus enhance material dependency: the direct influence of the care giver – just as that of the care receiver – on quality, extent, and the shaping of the work component diminishes as the caring relationship itself depends on other persons or institutions for support.

Material asymmetry partly inside and partly outside the caring relationship

A similar situation occurs where the resource component is located partly inside and partly outside the caring relationship. As the care giver and the care receiver depend on different sources for their support, the material dependency of the entire caring relationship is lessened since the dependency affects the care giver and the care receiver separately and presumably in varying intensities.

The material dependency of care receivers may have an influence on their demand for transactable caring services, that is, on the possibility for manifesting market demand if care receivers or their immediate (household) care givers lack access to and/or have only limited control of adequate resources to cover their demand on the market. Material dependency and the lack of control over financial resources may thus have the effect that the need for caring services, though real and continuous, does not always translate into market demand.

Resource control by care givers avoids their material dependency and opens up options for acquiring caring services on the market. It also enhances the care giver's sole power over the caring situation by bestowing on him/her not only physical but also economic power over the care receiver.

An instrument that can safeguard both parties from potential (economic) vulnerability are labor contracts that are clearly framed and legally enforceable as an exchange between care giver and care receiver. The danger of the care receiver's material dependency on the care giver can thereby be lessened. In like manner, the material situation of the care giver becomes more independent from the provider since the income of the care giver is regulated by the labor contract. The care giver is able to rely on a certain volume of income, whereas in more open contracts (e.g. marriage contracts) the care giver cannot ask for specific sums from the provider; the provider controls the financial resources. Moreover, with a labor contract working conditions can also be enforced to a considerable extent; the remunerated care giver therefore enjoys a greater scope of material independence. The general advantage offered by the coordination of dependency services via market exchange in the form of a labor contract is that the dangers of dependency, especially material dependency, are lessened, and (material) independence is increased. The existential dependency of the care receiver might also be lessened since she/he would no longer be subject to the arbitrary will of the care giver and would have some sort of enforceable certainty that certain dependency services will be performed.

It should be noted that caring situations provided within a single economic realm (e.g. the market) might still feature a range of structures dependent on the location of the resource component. The specific structure of a caring situation in which the care giver is hired, for example, depends on who pays for the care giver's wage – the care receiver or an outside provider – and, in the case of an outside provider, whether the outside provider is sustaining the care receiver as well. Consequently, when a caring service is procured on the market, the resource component may be located outside the work component as in child care where the parents buy the caring service for the child, or the resource component may be located within the caring relationship as in examples of elder care where the elderly person buys the caring service. The two structures have different impacts on material dependency for the care receiver. In the latter case, the care receiver, at least materially, can choose among alternative sources of care giving accessible with money.[7] In the first case, someone else, such as a close family member, purchases the caring service for the care receiver on the market. In these cases, the care receiver is materially dependent on a source outside the direct caring relationship. Only in caring situations where the care receiver pays for the service him/herself is there no outside determination of preferences and demand.

The crowding-out effect of material dependency

Keeping care givers materially dependent and, thereby, making it hard or impossible for them to exit from the caring situation is a measure that may

7 Rather than the financial resources of the care receiver, a voucher system would be conceivable to enable care receivers to make individual choices.

be used by some societal institutions as a means to ensure the performance of essential caring services. But no/low wages for care workers aggravates the material asymmetry between paid care givers and the provider. They put strains on the compensating power of the care workers' caring motivation, inducing the production of implicit labor grants, and giving others a free ride. Material dependency of the care giver, by this very circumstance, can result in the decline of the quality of caring since – in the absence of alternative material support – it may force those care givers to stay who would otherwise leave a caring situation. In this sense, low wages and material dependency of the care giver can exert a certain crowding-out effect to the detriment of the caring situation.

Low wages for highly motivated care givers can force some dependency workers to leave although they would prefer to stay. But they cannot afford to offset low wages and bad working conditions with caring motivation since they have to earn their living. This is reflected in the comparatively high turnover rates in dependency workers' jobs.[8] Some employed care givers must sustain families and therefore need a certain level of income. Accordingly, they leave caring situations and look for better paid jobs outside the caring sector.

Asymmetry in resource control and material dependency consequently have an effect on the extent to which functions are split and on the scope of choice for care giver and care receiver to decide how to organize the work component. The material status of care giver and care receiver may affect the market demand for caring services either by enabling giver or receiver to buy caring services in the market or by preventing them from doing so. And material dependency can exert a crowding-out effect on motivation.

Caring motivations and motivational barriers to exit

The earlier discussed asymmetry in capabilities and the existential dependency in the provision of caring services for dependents that structure the situation of the care receiver stand against the quite different situation on the part of the care giver. The structure on the demand side for dependency work makes the care receiver extremely vulnerable and – one should expect – the care giver potentially powerful. The dependent's special situation of neediness and vulnerability, the receiver's existential dependency on the care giver, contrasts with the care giver's command of

[8] Cf. the contributions in Nelson and Abel 1990 on the situation in the USA. Another reason for high turnover rates is that some people work as health aides because they have thus far been unable to find any other job. They leave the caring job as soon as they find work outside the sector. They are to be considered care laborers not care workers in Radin's sense.

exclusive power, her/his (at least momentarily) exclusive capability to perform the caring service. Strictly defined, the power that the care giver holds over the care receiver is a concrete physical power featuring superior capabilities and skills to perform the needed caring service.[9] It is of enormous social consequence for care giver and care receiver and is therefore also social power. Exclusive power, however, also means exclusive responsibility. It is here that we are faced with normative questions of social and economic justice, with equity issues, and with moral aspects, thus highlighting the importance of the social and ideological context.

The moral responsibility of the care giver

Caring motivations play a crucial role as strong forces in initiating and establishing caring relationships that lead to caring situations. Caring motivations ensure that caring services are provided even under difficult circumstances. There is, however, another aspect to caring motivations that becomes visible when the situation of the care giver is taken into (closer) consideration along with that of the receiver.

The existential dimension for the care receiver is a moral dimension of great responsibility for the care giver as reflected in the moral motivations to caring. In contrast to the dependent care receiver, the care giver generally has the option of entering into and exiting from caring situations. And yet, this option may still be limited in light of the existential dependency of the care receiver. Existential and material dependencies can create moral dilemmas and conflicts for the participants in a caring situation. (Sevenhuijsen 1998; Kittay 1999; Tronto 1993) This is all the more apparent the greater the existential need in question and the less capable of self-care the care receiver is. In particular with respect to caring for dependents where the life of the care receiver may be at stake, conflicts between the needs of the care receiver and the needs of the care giver reveal a deeply moral dilemma.

Care givers who care for dependents have an enormous responsibility to effectively perform an existentially needed caring service – in formal as well as informal situations. In the market, if an assembly line worker performs poorly, it is the worker's manager and the employer who assume accountability. By contrast, care givers who, as a result of detachment or failure of responsiveness to the dependent, allow the latter to take a step that should not have been taken, or fail to detect a dangerous rise in temperature, may be directly responsible for a serious illness or loss of life and be subject to enormous personal moral guilt. The same holds true for a dependency

---

[9] As is sadly apparent in cases of child and elder abuse. (Abel and Nelson 1990a: 25-26)

worker who exits from a caring situation for dependents without securing a replacement.

Caring motivations and sacrifice

The result of responsible caring behavior may be a non-exit situation for the dependency worker. Attending to the existential dependency of the care receiver might generate a motivational (or social) dependency of the care giver that takes the form of sacrifice. Alongside existential and material dependency, therefore, caring situations may exhibit a third kind of exit barrier in the form of the caring motivations of the persons involved; the superior power in the performance of caring activities may turn into a source of vulnerability for the care giver.

The exit desired or even already decided upon fails to take place because of the moral-motivational disposition of the care giver (such as a strong feeling of responsibility, sense of duty, or emotional attachment) fostered by the apparent asymmetry in the practical capabilities of caring which places a direct, special human responsibility upon the dependency worker. Moral considerations may well completely inhibit an exit. Exit is seen as uncaring. The stronger the caring motivation, the more difficult the exit. The more caringly motivated and engaged a person participating in a caring situation, the more difficult it will be for the person to leave the caring relationship.[10] Caring situations, therefore, feature a strong *producer loyalty*.

The argument of motivations preventing exit is also found in Albert Hirschman's deliberations on loyalty. (Hirschman 1970) Hirschman's concept of loyalty, though primarily focusing on *consumer* behavior vis-à-vis firms and organizations (in contrast to the *producer* behavior described here and involving the behavior of the care giver), can help to shed further light on the relationship between caring motivations and possibilities of exit from caring situations. With the help of Hirschman's concept of loyalty, caring motivations may be understood as "a force which in the act of postponing exit [...] may [...] save [care receivers] from the dangers of excessive or premature exit" (Hirschman 1970: 92). In the presence of caring motivations "spontaneous exit abruptly changes character: the applauded rational behavior of the alert participants in market transactions shifting to a better exchange situation becomes disgraceful desertion" (Hirschman 1970: 98). Caring motivations, therefore, render substantial the cost of exit. The penalty for leaving caring situations may be directly imposed as in the case of child neglect. In most cases, however, it is internalized.

---

[10] On organizations with high prices of exit see also Hirschman 1970: 96-97. On protection mechanisms of formal care givers with regard to this situation in the form of "detached attachment" see Nelson 1990: 217-224.

While loyalty postpones exit, Hirschman asserts that its very existence presupposes the possibility of exit, which in turn constitutes part of the loyal member's bargaining power vis-à-vis the organization. (Hirschman 1970: 82) In the case of caring for dependents, however, the dependency worker might not even have this as a last resort since the dependency worker's exit possibility takes on a special dimension. For leaving the dependency situation may mean the danger of death for the dependent care receiver who cannot survive without help.

Caring motivations also enable difficult caring situations to arise and continue. The motivational barrier to exit to some degree facilitates continuity and helps to guarantee the provision of a dependency service over time; this would be difficult to achieve in (exchange) situations where the barriers to exit are low. On the other hand, the beneficial outcome of caring motivations may also be non-optimal since caring motivations can overshoot the mark and turn into sacrifice in an undue neglect of the exit option.[11] Sacrifice, therefore, may be understood as a form of motivational dependency.

Sacrifice, as understood in this context, is a prolonged one-way transfer of caring services at the expense of the care giver's own self-care. Sacrificing behavior may reveal itself in a number of separate or combination of ways. It may result in the provision of more caring services than are needed, and in their provision at the expense of the care giver's own status of autonomy, i.e. in the provision of more caring services than the care giver's own situation can legitimately bear. Sacrifice may induce care givers to stay in exploitative caring situations since it may involve "mediating and nurturance skills that encourage [care givers] to identify with the interest of children, [spouses] or lovers, clients, patients and customers, thus making it difficult for [them] to take an oppositional stance of the sort necessary to acknowledge one's involvement in an exploitative exchange of labour." (Ferguson 1989: 97; see also Hochschild 1983: 150; Nelson 1990: 220, Himmelweit 1999: 35).

As problematic as pure self-interest may be, total sacrifice of oneself in consideration of others' needs is also not unproblematic. (Ulrich 1997: 62) Or as Julie Nelson notes, "the self-sacrificing [care giver] who simply reacts to any and all demands, regardless of cost, is guilty of being irresponsible to at least one human being in her (or his) care: herself (or himself)" (Nelson 1996: 71, Fn. 8). It is the balance between self-respect and charity, self-care and other-care, that is at stake here. The two poles of the caring spectrum

[11] According to Hirschman, loyalty might also "overshoot the mark and thus […] produce an exit-voice mix in which the exit option is unduly neglected" (Hirschman 1970: 92). Yet, in contrast to sacrifice, the exit barrier that results from loyalty is "of finite height (comparable to protective tariffs)" (Hirschman 1970: 79).

"caring for the self" and "caring for dependent others" are placed under a single roof in caring situations for dependents and show that the extreme nature of needs affect care receiver and care giver alike.

Derived vulnerability

While a small child is undoubtedly extremely vulnerable on the receiver's side, the caring person may indirectly be equally vulnerable with regard to his/her rather limited options to assign the work either temporarily or generally to someone else. In this sense, the neediness of other individuals can doubtless exert very strong social or individual power, particularly when it confronts the care giver disposing of a strong caring disposition. This situation may be one of the main reasons why, for example, there has never been a widespread, long-term strike by housewives or nurses. (see also Himmelweit 1999: 32 pp.)

When existential dependency meets real caring motivations that, together with societal value structures and rules and regulations, encourage responsible behavior and sanction irresponsible behavior toward dependents, the physical and social power of the dependency worker diminishes. Caring motivations, besides constituting the forces behind an entry into caring, also build social-psychological barriers to exit from caring situations and can even make it impossible for care givers to quit dependency situations. By the very situation of existential dependency, one might argue, the dependent care receiver exercises a powerful social-psychological influence over those involved in dependency situations, inducing them to sacrifice. But this power can only be exercised over the *caringly motivated* care giver and diminishes vis-à-vis less caring motivations to dependency work as they are commonly assumed, for example, in market transactions. When lacking personal and economic independence, care givers' generosity may turn against themselves. (Komter 1996b)

The vulnerability of the care receiver can thus be transferred to the care giver, whose inability to leave caring situations may result in her/his work being taken advantage of. The asymmetry that is found here is a *motivational* asymmetry between caring individuals and non-caring individuals within the caring situation itself, or between the participants of the caring situation and those outside, in society.

Interaction and mutual reinforcement of asymmetries and dependencies

As has been shown, asymmetries and dependencies inherent in caring situations for dependents decisively influence the structure of the need for and the provision of caring and dependency services. Moreover, asymmetries in the control of and access to resources, or in the motivation of the persons involved, even asymmetry in capabilities, can – in shades and degrees, temporarily or permanently – characterize every caring situation. They may influence both the choices of entry into and of exit from a dependency or caring situation – irrespectively whether the service in question is procured on the market or not.

Conceptualizing existential and material dependency and motivational exit barriers in such an analytically distinct manner does not mean that there are no combinations among the several types of dependency, that there are no interrelated dependencies, or that there are no variations or graduations of dependencies. Asymmetries and dependencies may interact and cumulatively reinforce one another, in extreme, though not infrequent, cases generating strong potential for personal conflict. The asymmetry in capabilities that is characteristic of caring situations for dependents may be enhanced by a parallel asymmetry in resource endowment between care giver and care receiver, or between the participants of the caring relation and the supporting person(s) or institution. This asymmetry influences the bargaining positions of both the care giver and care receiver and it can affect their choices as regards their respective entry into or exit from the caring relation.

Additional asymmetries may strengthen or diminish power. Very distinct existential dependency and material dependency may enhance the overall vulnerability of the care receiver. The asymmetry in capabilities underlying the existential dependency of the care receiver may be amplified by a parallel asymmetry in the control of and access to the resources needed to support the caring relationship creating material dependency. Motivational barriers to exit may in turn be triggered and reinforced by material dependency. On the other hand, the care giver's (exclusive) power of physical and mental capabilities and skills (not necessarily accompanied by economic power!) over the dependent may – theoretically and practically – be counterbalanced, weakened, and even offset by other asymmetries and dependencies possibly featured in caring situations such as the material dependency of the care giver on the care receiver. Changes in asymmetries in terms of capabilities (the work component) and material resource control (the resource component), and the resulting possible dependencies, have an impact on the caring motivation needed to bring about the performance of a dependency service (the motivation component).

Chapter 8

GUIDELINES FOR THE ANALYSIS OF CARING SITUATIONS IN ECONOMICS

As indicated in the introduction to Part III of this study, this last chapter is reserved for developing an integrated conceptual framework for the analysis of caring in economics that brings together the component concept of a caring situation as developed in Chapter 6 and the various types of asymmetries and dependencies that were systematized and analyzed in some detail in Chapter 7. With the help of this framework, sensitive points in the coordination and institutionalization of caring situations will be identified and directions for policy will be mapped out.

The integrated frame

The component concept is built on the insights developed in Part II of this study and put together with the analytical tools presented there. It takes account of existing theoretical approaches to caring in economics thus permitting their incorporation and integration into a common frame of reference. With the help of the component concept, all types of caring activities can be treated within a single analytical concept: caring for the self and caring for others, caring for dependents and caring among equally capable individuals. Perhaps even more significant is the fact that the concept adequately addresses the situation of caring for dependents, the theoretical bottleneck and test case of this study, and its specific characteristics.

Two-way asymmetries and dependencies

The social and economic organization of caring situations manifests itself in a variety of institutional structures in which the three components combine in a number of different ways. Almost all of the structures feature asymmetries and implicit or explicit dependencies of one kind or another; in caring situations for dependents these are inescapable circumstances. The combinations of the three components differ with respect to the extent to which they can deal with actual and possible asymmetries and dependencies inherent in caring situations. The analysis in Chapter 7 revealed that asymmetries and dependencies are characteristic of the structure of caring situations as proposed by the component concept. They operate in two directions:[1] (1) The structure of a caring situation may reflect and *be the result of* specific asymmetries and dependencies. (2) The structure of a caring situation may also *result in*, i.e. create or foster, specific asymmetries and dependencies. The structure of caring situations, therefore, reflects as well as influences the asymmetries and dependencies involved. Both aspects constitute decisive elements for further analysis.

(1) The previous analysis has shown that caring situations may be provided within different basic structures underlying institutional arrangements. These different structures of caring situations may reflect various types of impaired capabilities on the part of the care receiver, a range of circumstances with respect to material resource control, and the caring motivations of the people involved. The analytical structure of actual caring situations may have its origins in the care receiver's complete lack of autonomy and the division of functions which follow from it. Asymmetries and dependencies, their existence or non-existence, feed back into the interaction of the three components.

The component concept helps us identify and locate asymmetries, dependencies, and the workings of the underlying power structure that are created by the limited autonomy of the dependent care receiver. As was shown above (Chapter 7), asymmetries and dependencies in a caring situation may appear in different shapes, determined by the variable array of the respective components. *Asymmetry in capabilities* arises within the work component, whereas *material asymmetry* arises within both the work and the resource components. The components and their respective interaction help us specify and better understand the graduated scale on which the different kinds of asymmetries are located, and the ensuing (existential, material, and/or motivational) dependencies explicitly or implicitly involved especially in dependency situations.

The institutional arrangements in which caring for dependents is provided – whether in the informal or formal realm of the economy, whether the provider is a family member, friend, neighbor, government agency, government worker or a worker hired in the market – may be studied in terms of how they respond to asymmetries and dependencies, whether they alleviate or aggravate them. The component concept elaborates and makes possible the study of caring activities *across the different realms* of the economy within a common frame of reference. With the help of the analytical tools developed above, the social and economic institutions within which classic caring situations are provided can be analyzed in terms of the benefits and risks featured by the respective organization of caring situations.

---

[1] The two directions, of course, are interrelated. They are distinguished here for analytical purposes, but in actual caring situations they can intermingle.

(2) But not all asymmetries and dependencies in specific caring situations for dependents are the result of the characteristics of classic caring situations *per se*. The analytical structure of real-life caring situations may also be the result of a specific institutional arrangement by which (additional) asymmetries and dependencies are created, for example, with respect to the location of the resource component. In this case, asymmetries and dependencies are not necessarily connected to the care receiver's limited autonomy but are created or fostered by a specific social and economic organization of caring services, i.e. a specific combination of the three components. A prominent example would be the traditional bread-winner/ care-giver organization of the family where the work and the resource components are personally and fully divided, with the husband providing the resources and the wife in charge of performing the caring services, creating a material dependency of the care giver (and the caring relationship) on the provider.

The institutionalization of caring situations may create asymmetries by imposing time constraints on the performance of caring work. And taking time control away from the care giver may create an asymmetry affecting the resource component. The understaffing of nursing homes for the elderly may serve as an example. Here, the workload of the single dependency worker often prevents him/her from doing more than performing the instrumental tasks (at times a single dependency worker may have to attend to 30 care receivers during the day and to 60 care receivers at night). An asymmetry in time control is created between the provider/management and the care giver, forcing the care giver to concentrate on the instrumental aspects of caring services and neglect their communicative aspect.[2]

Changes in social structures affect the time allocated to caring. Full-time employment and limited opportunities for part-time work also put strains on the informal dependency worker's time control. Working hours in the formal realm determine the time left over for dependency work (if the informal care giver wants to remain employed). Employees with full-time jobs hardly have enough time left for the care receivers under their responsibility. The full-time employment of care givers in the formal realm results in a double burden for care givers, and in an asymmetry in time control between care givers and people outside caring relationships. With the increasing full employment of women, the time availability and the pool of these traditional care givers in society are shrinking. Consequently, some of the work, whether instrumental or communicative, may remain incomplete.

---

[2] As discussed below with respect to the rules and regulations of Germany's Long-Term Care Insurance.

The context of societal values and institutions

The degree of asymmetry involved in caring situations and the extent of dependency are thus shaped not only by the capacity of the care receiver for self-care, the critical nature of his/her needs, and the institutional organization of the access to and control of the resources needed to sustain a caring relationship as discussed above. They are also shaped by the larger context of societal values and institutions in which the caring is provided. Societal values and institutions may foster or hinder certain structures of caring situations (combinations of the three components). Besides confirming and aggravating inevitable asymmetries and dependencies, they create and enhance additional ones.

The ideological context not only plays an important role in shaping the institutionalization of caring institutions by helping determine what caring institutions are established or favored. Societal values and institutional arrangements may themselves act to enhance existing and create additional asymmetries and, therefore, possibilities for dependence. Societal values that are embodied in and expressed by institutions and, in turn, influence their shaping (Hodgson 1988: 123-144) may create asymmetries with broad impacts. This has an impact on asymmetries and dependencies between care giver and care receiver, between care givers and people outside dependency relationships, and between certain societal groupings. A devaluation of the performance of dependency work could, for example, result where dependent care receivers and their care workers are discriminated against or where caring responsibilities are assigned to a single group within society. The devaluation of care work leads to an asymmetry in social recognition between those who perform care work (or are looked upon to be responsible for care work) and those who do not. It is usually aggravated by discrimination against those who voluntarily or involuntarily undertake this work.[3] Needing and performing caring services for dependents still conflicts with the prevalent ideals of autonomy and independence.

The asymmetry in the social recognition of dependent care receivers and, more specifically, of their care workers can affect the organization of the resource component. The devaluation of care work may manifest itself in comparatively low wages for care givers, or the expectation that no wages at all should be paid for care giving.[4] The social devaluation of care work and discrimination against care givers are often seen in care givers' limited control of resources, be it through low wages for dependency work on the market or institutional arrangements (the traditional family) which strictly separate the work component from the resource component. Asymmetry in

---

[3] On the economic disadvantages of discrimination see Schubert 1993.

[4] On the evidence of and explanations for the "care penalty" see England and Folbre 1999a. Cf. also Nelson 2001.

recognition may result in inadequate attention to the special needs of dependent care receivers and result in the prolongation of asymmetries in capabilities and existential dependency. Examples may be found wherever there is a failure to provide adequate everyday infrastructure for people with walking or other motoric disabilities.

Societal values and institutions may influence the expectation of caring motivations and skills within certain groups in society thereby enhancing the possibility for other groups to free ride on the integrative products created.[5] The provision of caring services may be regarded as responsibility of certain groups in society. The expectation that dependency work is the task of a certain gender (women), class (the poor), race or ethnicity (minorities) operates in this direction. Although public discussion is trying to move away from these stereotypes and the "gendered inequality" (Himmelweit 1999: 31) in caring, and promote the sharing of caring responsibilities by men and women (Brouwer and Wierda 1998), statistical figures still show, for example, that women are more involved in caring jobs than men. (e.g. Folbre and Nelson 2000) Where political measures, such as Germany's Long-Term Care Insurance (Soziale Pflegeversicherung), encourage the performance of dependency work for the elderly within the family, it is women more often than men who do the job – not only because of their frequently lower opportunity costs in the market but also because they are considered to be more apt as care givers. As has been mentioned above, persons who care for dependent care receivers often encounter double burdens as well as other impediments.

Specifically evoking and socializing caring motivations in one group of society rather than another, and placing the responsibility for the performance of dependency services on one group in society rather than on others, contributes to an additional asymmetry. This is an asymmetry in motivation (with asymmetry in time and resource control as likely consequences) between care workers and those outside caring relationships for dependents, such as providers, or between care givers and those outside any caring situations for dependents, who live a life of "privileged irresponsibility" (Tronto 1993: 121).[6]

Devaluation of care work and discrimination against care givers, besides creating new asymmetries (and dependencies), aggravate already existing material and motivational dependencies on the part of the care giver since

---

[5] England and Folbre describe free-riders on caring performed by others as "the beneficiaries of caring labor, who extend beyond the actual recipients of the care" (England and Folbre 1999a: 45).

[6] Tronto argues that privileged irresponsibility is a "consequence of the unbalanced nature of caring roles and duties in our culture" (Tronto 1993: 120) and reflects the fact that some members of society have "the opportunity simply to ignore certain forms of hardships that they do not face" (Tronto 1993: 121).

they generally lower the possibility of voicing interests, weaken the bargaining power of care givers and care receivers, and limit their choices of exiting from exploitative caring situations. While such ideological arrangements might ensure that caring work "gets done," the circumstance of limited choice, and sometimes even compulsion by strict social sanctioning, are likely to have a diminishing impact on the caring motivation of the care giver.

Asymmetries induced by values and institutions such as the devaluation of care work and discrimination against care workers, thus clearly impede progress toward decreasing asymmetries and dependencies in the social organization of caring situations for dependents. This is a point to which we will return in the last section of this chapter.

Multilateral situations and split functions

By enabling an integrated study of the analytical perspectives of care receivers, care givers, and providers, the component concept sheds light on yet another (possible) characteristic of caring situations. The limited autonomy of the dependent care receiver and possible asymmetries and dependencies in resource endowment and control may lead to "split functions" ("Funktionstrennung," Herder-Dorneich 1980: 153) and the typical "non-market structure" (e.g. Herder-Dorneich 1980: 118) of caring situations. Split functions – i.e. the functions "identification of need," "voicing of need," and "resource control" are exercised by different persons – which characterize caring situations for dependents are not limited to the informal realm. The non-market structures of classical caring situations are also found in caring situations that are coordinated via the market.

Infants, mentally handicapped, or mentally confused elderly, for example, "seldom meet the standards for consumer sovereignty," (Folbre and Nelson 2000: 136); they are unable to exercise market demand in terms of both material resource control and their capability to enter market contracts. In these cases, market demand may be exercised by a person other than the care receiver: by the family or household care giver, for example, as in the case of parents demanding child care services. Also, the person demanding the service might not be the one controlling the resources to pay for it and might be materially dependent, lacking the financial resources to back up market demand. If, in addition, the dependency service is bought with the help of the provider, the functions of demanding, buying, and consuming the service are split. In such cases, the consumer is not an independent demander; rather, the demand is co-determined by the care giver and/or the provider. The care receiver has no influence on the amount or price of the caring services provided.

The assumption of autonomy in general exchange economics is therefore essentially an assumption of what might be called the *coincidence of functions*. Coinciding functions presuppose both the economic individual's mental autonomy to voice demand and his/her control of the financial resources to act on this demand. Yet, when the care receiver has only a limited capability to exercise market demand and enter market contracts, the commonly assumed coincidence of functions fails to apply even in market situations. Split functions reflect a situation in which the needs of the care receiver have to be identified by a second person and/or a person other than the care receiver controls the material and financial resources. The splitting of functions thus reflects both the care receiver's existential dependency and the material asymmetry among the persons involved in a caring situation. At the same time it augments the asymmetries and heightens the possibility of consequent dependencies of the care receiver on the care giver and on the provider of the resources. A specific institutional arrangement may also induce a splitting of functions.

Different coordination mechanisms

With regard to their coordination, caring situations characterized by split functions are multilateral one-way transfers rather than the bilateral two-way transfers characteristic of exchange situations. The task of coordination, therefore, requires the establishment of one-way transfers or "grants" (Boulding 1973: 1). Different forms of coordination can deal with asymmetries and dependencies and coordinate one-way transfers in a number of ways and to various extents. Caring services, at a basic level, may be provided within grant relationships or exchange relationships. Three broad forms of coordination and their benefits and risks with respect to caring situations will be sketched in the following: gift-giving, reciprocity, and exchange. Because of their ability to deal with asymmetries and organize one-way transfers, gift giving and reciprocity take on special importance (vis-à-vis exchange) with respect to the coordination of (classic) caring situations.[7]

Gift giving: The organization of caring relationships as gift relationships has many advantages. Yet, it also involves a number of risks and shortcomings that largely serve to reinforce and reinstate asymmetries and dependencies and add additional ones. In gift relationships, there is commonly no negotiation of the terms of trade; more specifically, there is no possibility for the care receiver either to influence the terms of the one-way transfer or change or reinforce them. The motivation of the care giver is the decisive element; the care receiver is dependent on the care giver for any

---

[7] For an overview of additional forms of coordination see e.g. Dahl and Lindblom 1953.

spontaneous changes in the flow of the one-way transfers. This can be difficult to accept. The dependent state of the care receiver defines her/his limited scope for real choice as to the extent, frequency, or kind of caring service provided.

According to Boulding, grants "almost always imply a superior status of the grantor to the recipient" (Boulding 1973: 22; see also Boulding 1978: 192-193). Complex secondary reactions on the part of the care receiver such as regretting both the actual costs and the opportunity costs incurred by the giver, or the obligation for gratitude, might further constrain the care receiver in his/her relations to the care giver. (Sahlins 1974: 207-208) Although this effect may be somewhat less in the case of reciprocal grants, it is especially pronounced in gift relationships.

Reciprocity: Reciprocal grant relationships also have their risks and shortcomings. Although reciprocity may be viewed as a constructive element in social interactions and social systems, particularly in their establishment and cohesion, it may also foster dysfunctions and induce tensions. The fact that obligations of reciprocity are normally imposed only when the individual has the capacity to do so, for example, presupposes agreement on the individual's capabilities. And there might also be doubts about whether the individual's return is appropriate or sufficient (apart from whether it is equivalent). Strategic expectations of reciprocity might lead individuals to establish caring relations only or primarily with those who are able to reciprocate,[8] thus risking the neglect of the needs of those unable to do so. Reciprocity thus acts not only as a mechanism of inclusion, fostering cohesion within the community, but also as a principle of exclusion.[9]

This element of exclusion in the integrative power of caring services organized as gift relationships or reciprocal grant relationships must be recognized when advocating the use of reciprocity to coordinate caring relationships for dependents or provide caring services as labor grants given as gifts. The production of the integrative product with some care receivers might work to exclude others, and the integration of some individuals might be a means of oppressing those who are excluded.[10] Gift giving and the coordination of grants by reciprocity therefore require political, legal, and social frameworks to help avoid these risks.

---

[8] Cf. Chapter 5 on experimental models of altruistic behavior and intention-based reciprocity.

[9] Komter argues that people who live in difficult social and economic circumstances, such as the unemployed and most elderly, are likely to face increasing disintegration of their social relations. This, in turn, is very likely reflected in their also being the poorest recipients in reciprocal gift giving. (Komter 1996: 7; 1996a)

[10] Historically, social security systems and charity were aimed at those who were excluded from informal and formal communities.

There might be another danger involved in the provision of caring services as one-way transfers. Most caring services for dependents, such as child care or care for the sick and disabled, seek to render the dependent as autonomous as possible. But the dependency worker might purposely perform the service longer than needed, that is, long after the dependent has acquired the capacity of self-care. By prolonging the relationship, the care giver, whether intentionally or unintentionally, continues to exercise psychological, social, economic, or political power. In such cases, caring services for dependents might prolong dependency or create new forms of it.

The imbalance of power inherent in grant relationships, whether gift or reciprocal relationships, may consequently become detrimental to the caring situation in several respects: by turning the grant relationship into an exploitative relationship, by turning the integrative relationship into one of exclusion, or by reinforcing and prolonging the care receiver's existential dependency.

Exchange: At a conceptual level, exchange relationships reduce at least some of the risks and shortcomings of grant relationships. Exchange is conceptualized as a two-way transfer of economic goods and services. Unlike a pair of mutual grants as found in reciprocity, these transfers are conditional. If the transactions amount to a simple exchange, the terms of trade can be negotiated. Since the assumption is that exchange is voluntary and uncoerced and takes place only if both parties benefit, "exchange, almost by its very symmetry, implies equality of status." (Boulding 1973: 26) Exchange relationships therefore constitute a possible escape from the inequality status inherent in grant relationships. By conceptual assumption, the monopoly of the care giver is neutralized via the market. By offering money in return for a caring service within a labor contract, the care receiver does not become indebted and is not under obligation to the care giver or the subordinate recipient who receives favors from the care giver. The care giver, on the other hand, receives material income. The labor contract, clearly framed as enforceable terms of trade for care giver and care receiver, counteracts the possible (economic) vulnerability of both parties. These advantages of (market) exchange relationships, however, are accompanied by the risk of commodification and alienation and are provided at the possible expense of the integrative product. But in the case of caring situations for dependents, even the exchange mechanism is unable to offset such relationships' characteristic non-market structure. The exchange mechanism and its advantages are thus not applicable (at least conceptually) to all caring situations.[11]

[11] On advantages and disadvantages of market alternatives to informal family care see also Folbre and Nelson 2000; Nelson and England 2002; Held 2002. On labor contracts as partial gift exchange see Akerlof 1982.

Does this discussion then end with the well-known market versus non-market controversy with respect to the provision of caring services? After all, there is no guarantee with respect to any of the three coordination mechanisms. The above analysis and the short sketches on coordination mechanisms would instead suggest that the questions to be asked extend beyond or lie before it. Whether paid or unpaid, provided via the market or in the informal realm of the economy, the question is not so much whether one specific mechanism of coordination is to be favored over another. What must be carefully considered is the degree to which asymmetries and dependencies are created, reinforced, or continued by specific institutional arrangements, independent of the realm of the economy in which they are provided. Asymmetries and dependencies are a product of the bodily and mental conditions of the care receiver, and of concrete political and historical settings.

Accordingly, a significant feature of any institution, whether it be family structures, a commercial nursing home, state provision, or a neighborhood help system, is the manner (combination) in which these different institutional arrangements of caring situations bring together the work, resource, and motivation components. And more specifically, how, in doing so, these institutional arrangements address the main features of a caring situation, that is, how the specific institutional arrangement deals with the asymmetries involved, whether it enhances them, and whether it alleviates or aggravates the existential, material, and motivational dependencies involved. Does a specific institutional arrangement or, on a more general level, does public policy responsibly deal with the inevitable asymmetries and dependencies? Does it avoid aggravating them? Does it create additional ones?

The hypothesis of this study is that scope is available to avoid many of these institutionally induced or aggravated asymmetries and dependencies, and that the task of any long-term sustainable social and economic organization of caring situations may be described at a very general level as the task of effectively combining the motivation, work, and resource components of caring situations in such a way as to minimize asymmetry and dependency between the persons involved.

Sensitive points in the coordination and institutionalization of caring situations

Against the conceptual background of this study and with the help of the analytical tools presented and developed above a number of dilemmas may be identified in the provision of caring. They reveal what could be called *sensitive points* in the coordination and institutionalization of caring situations. Together with the asymmetries and dependencies above, they constitute further points of reference for the social and economic organization of caring services.

The sensitive points in the social and economic organization of caring situations as systematized in the following reflect the different aspects of caring outlined in the previous chapters. Some of these points are an expression as well as a result of the asymmetries and dependencies involved in caring and reflect the difficulties in responsibly addressing these aspects; others reflect the imperatives of the component model. The sensitive points discussed in the following are: the split between instrumental and communicative caring tasks, stratification, and balancing care givers' and care receivers' needs. They are interrelated and at times mutually reinforcing.

Splitting instrumental caring tasks from communicative caring tasks

The split between instrumental and communicative caring tasks as discussed in Chapter 5, acts as a field of tension between the tendency to commodify caring services, reducing them only to their instrumental and commodity aspects, and the aim of and need for producing the integrative product. The tension arises from splitting the work component and the motivation component, from adopting a commodifying view of caring services.

Commodification is the result of a one-sided attempt to quantify, commercialize, and economize caring services by concentrating only on the instrumental dimension of these activities, by "measuring" quality as if it were quantity. But caring involves characteristics that do not offer the conditions for commodification: these features are not easily quantifiable (e.g. listening, loving, etc.), made operational (e.g. giving a feeling of security, trust, etc.), or observable at any moment in time. The communicative dimension of caring is difficult to operationalize and quantify. (see also Himmelweit 1999: 37) This is, consequently, also true for the integrative product as a quality binding the instrumental and communicative parts of caring. In the process of commodifying caring services, essential quality is thus lost.[12] To take a predominantly commodifying view of caring services is therefore generally considered to be "uncaring." In other words, the commodification of caring services is contested[13] and incomplete[14].

---

[12] Caring services, therefore, are a very striking example of the difficulties that arise when the attempt is made to integrate services in general (as different from goods) into economic theorizing. (e.g. Rifkin 1995)

[13] "Contested commodification" reflects that fact that there is personal and social conflict regarding the process and result of commodification, that is, whether anything valued *can* be commodified and, if commodification is possible, whether it *should* be commodified.

Commodification, albeit a precondition for transactions of market exchange, is by no means restricted to them; commodification can also occur in other institutional settings. Triggered by financial considerations and budget constraints, political measures continue to force the managements of caring institutions into the commodification of caring services. The new system of accounting under Long-Term Care Insurance in Germany, for example, requires a precise accounting of the instrumental services provided and allots no room for a listing of the communicative part of caring. Moreover, the additional administrative work required of nurses further reduces care givers' time for communication with care receivers.[15] Rules and regulations in this case encourage and reinforce behavior that if exhibited by care givers on their own accord would be considered inappropriate and uncaring; for the general expectation is that care givers should make up for the lack of caring motivations in providers, whether they be nursing homes or families. The commodification of caring services, therefore, may lead to a distorted valuation of caring and set the wrong incentives for an "efficient" handling of the issues involved in the social and economic organization of caring services.[16] This principal risk resulting from the commodification of caring services not only applies to caring services that are coordinated via the market but also to those that are performed in other realms of the economy.

The relation between the instrumental and the communicative parts of caring also plays a role in the context of the discussion on greater professionalization in the performance of caring, and especially of dependency services. This discussion is characterized by different understandings of professionalization with respect to caring work. On the one hand, professionalization is seen as focusing on the instrumental part of caring and resulting in greater instrumental specialization and more administration.[17] On the other hand, professionalization along these lines is viewed with skepticism by professional dependency workers. Studies show that they understand the professionalization of their work to entail, alongside instrumental skills, greater emphasis and scope for the communicative side of caring, which they perceive as decisive for quality

The possibility as well as the desirability of commodification can be contested. (Radin 1996)

[14] Radin develops the notion of "incomplete commodification" conceiving commodification "as a matter of degree" (Radin 1996: 115).

[15] For the accounting procedures see Soziale Pflegeversicherung mit Nebenbestimmungen. SGB XI. 1996.

[16] Cf. Jochimsen 1994: 28-37.

[17] An example is the accounting system behind Germany's Long-Term Care Insurance. For an example of the consequences of accounting systems in an American nursing home for Medicaid recipients see e.g. Diamond 1990: 183-184.

care. They view professionalization as meaning more opportunities to focus on relational and integrative aspects of their work. The communicative part is of vital importance for the joy they derive from their work and work performance. (Brodkin Sacks 1990: 188-189) When the communicative side of caring is cut by external constraints such as time limits, leaving hardly any opportunity to establish a communicative relationship with persons in their care, care givers react by complaining that their interest in the work as such diminishes.[18]

A concept of professionalization that produces a splitting of caring work into its instrumental and communicative parts, forcing the *professional* care workers (e.g. nurses in nursing homes) by external constraints to focus on the instrumental part of caring and *non-professionals* (e.g. visiting family members or volunteer care workers) to focus on the communicative side, risks the unintentional and undesirable crowding-out effect of caring motivation in professional care givers. And it may lead to a (further) reduction in their pool. At the same time, it entails an outsourcing of the communicative part, increasing the demand for non-professionals to attend to this side of caring, in itself only a fraction of the package.

In the context of the integrated concept of caring as put forward in this study, any specialization and splitting of caring into instrumental and communicative parts is considered counterproductive, since it is the instrumental and the communicative parts *taken together* that produce the integrative product. The splitting of instrumental and communicative caring tasks and their assignment to different categories of care givers does not bring about the integrative product; it reduces the amount of "real caring" offered. Such a development is not an inevitable side effect of the professionalization of caring work. But it is characteristic of the prevalent concept of professionalization and its materialization.[19]

Stratification

The task of the social and economic organization of caring situations is further complicated by the different starting positions of care receivers and care givers. Stratification is found in both groups. Moreover, a gap separates those who are inside dependency situations from those on the outside. There are four basic types of stratification which will be sketched in the following:

---

[18] Time constraints may also often leave professional dependency workers in administrative positions without any contact to care receivers. Furthermore, professional dependency workers doubt that greater professionalization thus understood is helpful in nurturing caring dispositions. (Nelson 1990: 213)

[19] The split of instrumental and communicative tasks in caring here is identified as a general tendency. This is not to say that dependency workers who primarily perform instrumental tasks or are forced to do so by time shortage are uncaring. It merely shows the impact that these developments might have on the production of the integrative product.

stratification in the group of care givers manifests itself in care workers' skills. The group of care receivers may be stratified according to the limitations of their capabilities and the extent of their resource control. Both groups may be stratified with respect to the respective social context available to them. Stratification by gender, class, caste, and ethnicity cuts across all four types.

Stratification with respect to skills: when we look at the group of care givers, we see that their status is "far from uniform" (Abel and Nelson 1990a: 15). The need for special skills for the care of dependent children, the sick and disabled, and elderly care receivers induces stratification within the group of care givers by increasing the asymmetry between unskilled and skilled care givers in both the formal and informal realms. In the formal realm, it may contribute to higher pay for skilled dependency workers since their training requires time and resources, boosting their cost and wages – and even lower pay for the unskilled.

The need for better trained and more highly qualified dependency workers also has an impact on the possible contribution of "unskilled" voluntary labor in the informal realm in meeting the increasing needs, especially in the case of elder care. Since the task of performing caring services for the dependent elderly is becoming more and more complicated, it is getting increasingly difficult for dependency workers in families and for charitable volunteers to perform the task. At the same time, the workload and limited time of care givers employed in the formal realms are making it necessary for them to be supported by informal care givers. Dependency workers in nursing homes, for example, often rely on support by families of care receivers (cf. Bowers 1990) and by groups in civil society. The workload is divided into a more instrumental part for the formal dependency worker and a more communicative part for the family or social groups member. This development is being reinforced by the fact that the differentiation in the degrees of existential dependency continues to increase, a consequence being that dependency workers in nursing homes for the elderly very often attend only to the severest cases. This strengthens the tendency to further separate the more instrumental caring tasks from the more communicative caring tasks, respectively assigning them to skilled formal care workers and unskilled informal care workers.

In the informal realm these trends may lead to the need for getting skilled help from outside the family. Elderly persons who cannot afford skilled professionals, either because of a lack of resources or because their insurance does not provide such benefits will most likely have to fall back on more affordable arrangements. These may entail the use of informal and unskilled dependency workers. And there is very likely to be greater reliance on dependency workers from abroad, skilled (as in the case of foreign nurses working as health aides) or unskilled dependency workers who are willing to work for lower wages in the formal market or in black markets. Both solutions have their pitfalls. If skilled workers are the only ones able to provide adequate dependency care, the unskilled care givers may endanger the well-being of the care receiver. And the hiring of skilled care givers at lower wages and most likely under vague contract conditions without fringe benefits may violate considerations of care giver equity. Such arrangements, if they lack official permission, make both the work and the workers illegal. Neither the reliance on voluntary (unskilled) help nor on skilled dependency workers, if underpaid and/or illegal, can provide long-term solutions to the problem.

Stratification with respect to capabilities: this type of stratification is best exemplified in relation to the social and economic organization of dependency situations for the elderly. Besides its topical relevance in the political debate, care for the elderly is an area that is especially interesting since, unlike the situation in child care, the elderly care receiver is a person who in most cases was once autonomous and independent in the sense of market exchange economics but in the last part of life faces various impairments of autonomy and is subject to dependencies. Also unlike children, elderly people may be materially independent of their care givers and others. The kind and degree of the existential dependencies vary according to the mental and physical constitution (stratification with respect to capabilities), the financial situation (stratification with respect to resource control), and the social context (stratification with respect to the availability of caringly motivated care givers) of the elderly person.

Some elderly care receivers, though frail and dependent on help for the performance of daily activities such as dressing, washing, or walking, may still be capable of demanding and purchasing dependency services (provided their financial status allows them to do so). Others, though physically able to perform certain activities of self-care, may not be able to participate in market transactions because of their mental state of health. Just as varied as their needs, and the kinds of caring services required to meet them, are the institutional arrangements that exist. It therefore makes sense, to resort to the concept of choice in this context.

Stratification with respect to resource control: there is a stratification within the group of the elderly not only in terms of capabilities but also in material resource control which is not the result of mental capabilities but of a lack of material resources. The cultural and social minimum costs continue their rapid acceleration as a consequence of the increase in the division of labor, commodification, commercialization, and similar developments, as well as the ongoing shrinkage in the self-provision of material needs. Yet, although an impressive number of the elderly are comparably well-off, a large portion (mostly women) still face old-age poverty. Furthermore, the steep rise in health costs leaves an even larger part of the population without the financial and material means to respond to rising dependency needs. Whereas some elderly people can afford high quality care organized in a private context, in the family, at home, or in a private nursing home, others have to rely on public institutions. The strong and increasing (economic) interest in the purchasing power of the better-off and still healthy young elderly stands against a lack of interest in the poorer, less able, older elderly. (Hoskins 1993: 347)

As has been discussed in Chapter 7, the lack of resource control, whether as the result of poverty, material dependency on an outside provider, or owing to limited mental abilities, has important implications for the choice of alternative caring situations, in most cases with a limiting impact. The possibility of opting for alternative ways of organizing dependency situations, by hiring a care worker, for example, is thus reduced.

Stratification with respect to the social context: the choice between care for the elderly in a state or private nursing home, and care within the family, however, depends on more than just the availability of material resources. It also depends on the respective degree of family embeddedness of the elderly person. Some elderly may have families to help them, while others have to rely entirely on non-family help. Changing family structures, increasing female employment, and considerable living distances among (extended) family members render care within the family difficult. But even if the elderly person does not live in the family, its support is needed for both communicative and instrumental caring tasks. Elderly persons who are backed by a caring family are much better equipped to deal with non-family caring institutions.

The stratification of the elderly into groups of dependent and not-yet-dependent elderly, the better off and the poor, those who have families to care for them and those who do not, to name but a few, is an important characteristic of the current trends that public policy makers must keep in mind. (cf. Ottnad 2000: 277) What might be expected of one group in terms of material input or choice between different caring institutions cannot necessarily be generalized and extended to the respective other group. This situation points to the desirability of a diversified landscape of caring institutions.

Balancing care givers' and care receivers' needs

Another sensitive point in the coordination and institutionalization of caring situations for the elderly is the potential tension between the need to provide dependency services and interests of self-care; between the poles of concern for others and goals of self-realization; between the needs, interests, and legitimate claims of the dependent elderly care receivers and the interests of their (possible) care givers.

Self-care and other-care: Care for others and care for the self are strongly interlinked. It is helpful to look at self-care, own-account caring services, and non-service caring activities when trying to obtain a comprehensive understanding of the general provision of caring activities. An aim of other-regarding caring activities is to render the care receiver capable of self-care wherever possible: both in general and in the physical, mental, vocational, and family contexts. The ultimate goal of child care and of the rehabilitation and care for the (temporarily or permanently) disabled is to render care receivers (again) capable of self-care, as with care for the sick; or at encouraging, retaining, or restoring as much capacity for self-care as possible, as in care for the elderly. Furthermore, caring for others presupposes a minimum amount of self-care by the care giver. This is a practical necessity, and room must be left for it if other-regarding caring is to be provided in the medium-to-long terms. Whatever the institutional arrangements of caring for others, they must allow the care giver enough room for self-care (restoration, rehabilitation, leisure time, and participating in society) if he/she is to provide other-care over a longer period of time.[20] The argument for self-care highlights the (existential) needs of the care giver, which must also be given due recognition and consideration in discussions that normally address only the needs of the care receiver. Through self-care considerations we are forced to address social justice and equity concerns.[21]

Self-realization versus concern for others in civic involvement: The differing interests posed by the concern for others and goals of self-realization also play a role in terms of the future contribution of civic involvement in the provision of caring for the dependent elderly. Public discussions on care for the elderly, for example, repeatedly stress the importance of voluntarism in this field, expressing the hope that labor grants by volunteer care workers can help fill the gap of care workers needed.

But present developments indicate quite a different tendency. Robert Putnam, for example, studied societal trends in the United States and measured the degree of volunteer contributions to civil society via the participation of individuals in associations and the performance of labor grants. His study suggests that civic involvement in the United States has generally suffered from an overall decline over the past two decades. (Putnam 1995; Putnam 2000: Section II) For Germany, on the other hand, available data did not confirm such a reduction in general civic

---

[20] Cf. also Kittay's concept of "doulia" which states that a person caring for dependents is entitled not to a reciprocal act from the dependent care receiver, but to a sustaining relationship for her/himself. (Kittay 1999: 68)

[21] It would be very productive and desirable to study and conceptualize the relationship between self-care and other-care in more detail – a task, however, not to be undertaken at this point and in this investigation.

commitment.[22] (Ottnad, Wahl and Miegel 2000: 207) Yet the studies indicate a change in the motivations for volunteer contributions, and in what volunteers expect when they provide labor grants. They indicate a shift in civic involvement away from church and religiously oriented associations, which provide substantial caring and dependency services, to the benefit of the so-called "fun domains" (sports, play and leisure activities) (Zimmer and Priller 1997: 260-261), along with a shift from more continuous involvement, which is so important for caring situations, to the performance of more sporadic labor grants (Ottnad, Wahl and Miegel 2000: 207). When asked for their reasons for engaging in volunteer work, individuals generally stressed that their volunteer activity should contribute to their personal self-fulfillment and self-realization, rather than stating their concern for others. (Zimmer and Priller 1997: 251)[23] The percentage of those volunteering out of other-regarding motives is continuously shrinking.

The motivations of self-fulfillment and personal joy which inspire civic involvement clearly differ from those motivations that we identified as caring motivations and discussed in Part II of this study. At first glance, self-fulfillment and self-realization as caring motivations would seem to contradict concern for others since the former are centered around the care giver and the latter focuses more closely on the care receiver. But goals of identity could be reconciled with goals of concern if all members of society were to view caring as part of their self-realization, if concern and caring for others became part of an individual's identity, reflecting the strong public-good dimension of caring.

But civic involvement in caring situations also depends on other conditions being met. One prerequisite is naturally that those members of society who are expected to perform one-way transfers, or at least to temporarily waive a return for their services, must (materially and skill wise) be able to do so: the motivation, work, and resource components have to be combined. Volunteer care workers need more than motivation. They also require the time and skills to perform caring services. And they need material resources to (at least) sustain themselves and their families. Otherwise they have no basis from which to give labor grants.[24] From this perspective, other-care presupposes self-care. And the question is how to foster and induce caring motivations while ensuring the possibility of self-care (e.g. via working conditions, appropriate time allotment, social and

---

[22] The major sources are the Socio-economic Panel and the Johns Hopkins Comparative Nonprofit Sector Project.

[23] At the same time, the scope for civic involvement with respect to care for the elderly is not yet fully explored and organizational efforts could be increased. (Evers 2001: 89)

[24] Thus, policies such as granting tax benefits to foster civic involvement in caring would serve not necessarily as incentives to dependency work but would help to ensure the material basis for caring motivations to operate on.

financial recognition, time for recreation) and inhibiting the care giver's tendency to sacrifice and become vulnerable to exploitation. (cf. Fraser 1997)

Caring motivations and mandated civic service: On the one hand, elderly care receivers have a legitimate claim to quality care: this claim derives from issues of human respect and dignity. And nowadays it is also a very real material consequence of the contributions that elderly persons paid into social insurance over the years. On the other hand, the "most caring" caring services are provided from intrinsic motivations. (see Chapter 5) However, in view of the present crisis with regard to the provision of caring services, it might not be either possible only to create gift relationships, or affordable to force the establishment of exchange relationships. Might, therefore, social policy have to resort to compulsory labor-grant relationships,[25] at least for a limited time and extent? Could one possibility in this context be the introduction of a mandatory caring service period as citizens' duty? Straightforward compulsion, however, is not likely to foster the quality of caring since it may crowd-out caring motivations.[26] On the other hand, the entirely voluntary provision of caring services constitutes an ongoing risk for care receivers. Should such mandatory measures be necessary, equity concerns would have to be observed in their organization and the creation of additional asymmetry would have to be avoided. Only if this were done could such a mandatory service period be legitimized and an increase in caring motivations made more likely.

In striking a balance between the needs of the care giver and the care receiver the task is to ensure that the care receiver's legitimate claim to quality caring services is satisfied while the care givers' claims to self-care and the possible counterproductive effects of compulsion on the care giver's motivation are responsibly addressed.

Directions for policy

The aim of this study has been to develop a heuristic framework for the analysis of a central problem of public policy, guiding us through this theoretically open field: It has not been undertaken to suggest specific policy measures. The hypotheses advanced are elaborated and developed from the specific conceptual approach taken. They deal with the

---

[25] A "negative grant" belonging to a "threat system" (Boulding 1973: 22) also results in a one-way transfer. A threat relationship, in this sense, bears the same formal setup as the gift relationship stemming from benevolence – but the motivations for the grant differ.

[26] Cf. Chapter 5 on the possibility of crowding-out intrinsic motivation under specific external circumstances.

prerequisites for the organization of effective caring situations for dependents in present-day societies.

Coordinates for the social and economic organization of caring situations

Caring situations have been conceptualized as consisting of the simultaneous presence of a motivation, a work, and a resource component. The most decisive asymmetries and dependencies likely to be involved in classical caring situations have been outlined. They form the central categories for analysis and main coordinates for the social and economic organization of caring situations. They include the limited capabilities of the care receiver and existential or life-sustaining nature of the caring needs (degree of existential dependency); the institutional organization of the access to and control of resources (degree of material dependency), and the balance between other-care and self-care (motivational barriers to exit and risk of sacrifice). (Chapter 7)

The task of care-oriented policies has been found to be two-fold: a) to deal responsibly with inevitable asymmetries and dependencies and b) to avoid the creation of additional ones, i.e. to minimize asymmetries and dependencies in caring situations. The task is thus to help create caring situations that appropriately respond to the actual/potential asymmetries and dependencies likely to be involved in the provision of caring services. This should be done in such a way that the respective institutional arrangement of the work, resource, and motivation components avoids the creation, manifestation, or prolongation of existing or additional dependencies of care receivers and care givers.

On the basis of the analysis and with the help of the analytical tools presented and developed, the study has also been able to identify a set of sensitive points in the social and economic organization of caring in addition to the asymmetries induced by societal values: the splitting up of communicative and instrumental caring tasks, stratification in the group of care givers and in the group of (dependent) care receivers, and self-realization versus concern for others.

Taking our discussion one step further, it could be argued that from this perspective the characteristics of caring (the limited autonomy of the care receiver, the types of asymmetries and dependencies involved, split functions, and the prominence of one-way transfers) not only constitute central categories of analysis; they also influence and shape the structure of caring situations. Because of their decisive impact on the social organization of caring situations they may also be understood as major coordinates in the social and economic organization of caring situations. The sensitive points discussed in the previous chapter are to be added to this set of coordinates.

Account must be taken of both in the social and economic organization of caring situations for dependents.

It would be beyond the scope and aim of this study to propose solutions with respect to the present situation and the need for providing caring in postindustrial service societies. As was argued above, any useful inquiry into these matters must take the context in which caring situations are provided into account and seek to understand how caring situations are accomplished in concrete political and historical settings. With respect to the fields of tension, however, we can suggest two major directions in which socio-economic policy should be encouraged: one is to open up possibilities for exit and choice for persons inside non-voluntary caring situations for dependents, enabling care givers and care receivers to leave exploitive relationships; the second is to encourage persons outside caring situations for dependents to actively participate in such situations. The hypothesis is that this would a) act as further encouragement in the interest of a diversified landscape of caring institutions of comparable (high) quality and b) represent additional steps toward addressing equity concerns relating to care givers and care receivers. Measures to inhibit a (premature) exit from caring situations for dependents would thus be paralleled by policies to foster the entry of potential care givers now outside caring situations.

Fostering a diversified landscape of caring institutions

At present, caring situations are provided by a plurality of institutions in the private sector of personal living structures (family), in the market, in society, and in the public sector. The social and economic organization of caring situations is therefore characterized by an institutional mix of one-way transfers and two-way transfers, that is, of gift and mutual grant as well as exchange relationships. Care for the elderly and care for small children, for example, are achieved in a variety and combination of different caring situations: a family member, a hired care giver, and/or a volunteer care worker; sometimes a nurse or kindergarten teacher perform the needed dependency services. No single coordination mechanism can ordinarily solve the overall problem nor can a single economic realm normally assume all responsibility.

Ideally, this brings together the respective advantages of each of the different relationships while mutually offsetting their risks and shortcomings. But the opposite may also occur, with the respective pitfalls amplifying one another and the benefits being offset. Yet the answer to problems involving the social organization of dependency work is not always the replacement of one coordination mechanism by another or, to avoid the traps presented by grant relationships, their conversion into exchange relationships, or vice versa. Rather, the solution centers on the quality of different caring situations in different economic domains and on helping persons find their individual institutional mix for the required dependency services.

For choice to be a reality, however, there must be qualitatively comparable alternatives to choose from. This, of course, is a matter not only of material aspects (i.e. the choice of hired dependency workers or a bed in nursing homes of different qualities, etc.), but also of the general availability of various types of dependency workers and dependency situations: family, friends, society, market.

Dependent individuals, of course, must be equipped with the opportunity to access the different institutional arrangements and to make a real choice. Access, here, is to be understood in two different respects. First, and in the present situation very important, it means access to the material and financial resources which are key to such a choice. The material stratification within the group of the elderly as described above must be considered, and equity concerns as well as the just distribution of care provision must be ensured. Second, and of increasing importance, it also means access to social networks, to families, friends, and society. Only if dependent individuals are part of the social environments and communities in which they live will they have a real option for grant relationships in obtaining dependency services. Furthermore, as not all care receivers can themselves monitor quality or have family members or friends do so, minimum standards (e.g. the size of rooms in nursing homes) and quality control take on a role of central importance. (cf. also Folbre and Nelson 2000: 136)

Questions of the evaluation and right proportion of grants and exchange thus arise not only at a societal[27] or sectoral[28] level. They also and very specifically arise at the individual level since grant relationships and market

[27] According to Boulding, the proper balance or, as he himself puts it, the "proper boundary between the 'exchange economy' and the 'grants economy'" (Boulding 1973: 63), the "problem of the right proportions and the interactions of the [two]" (Boulding 1973: 9) and, accordingly, the consequent use of all three social organizers (love, fear, exchange) is "perhaps the most important question in political economics" (Boulding 1973: 9). Finding the right answer to this question presupposes that exchange and grant economies are seen as "equal partners in the total social enterprise" (Boulding 1973: 13).

[28] The production of public health in some countries is an example for a plurality of coordination mechanisms working together in the production of a particular good. The German public health sector, for example, is characterized by multiple coordination (Vielfachsteuerung). Markets are of marginal importance; central planning and administration play a subordinate role; group negotiations, voting, and exchange against vouchers dominate. (Herder-Dorneich 1980: 152) Health economics analyzes which coordination mechanisms secure optimal provision for which dimensions of health goods. Herder-Dorneich asserts that, in the end, there will always be multiple modes of coordination. (Herder-Dorneich 1980: 21)

exchange relationships combine in the lives of individuals in the provision of caring services for the dependent elderly. The actual institutional mixes may be very situation-specific and depend on the individuals' evaluation of the grant and exchange relationships offered. In fact, a plurality of coordination mechanisms must work together.

A diversified landscape of caring institutions is thus favorable and must be encouraged, not only to share the increasing work load and responsibility for its performance, but also to enhance dependents' individual choices for the kind and mix of caring situations which best suit them.[29] A plurality of caring institutions of comparable quality in caring for dependents would be able to respond adequately to the stratification outlined above. For it would address issues of choice, individuality, and stratification, and thus open up new fields of cooperation among individuals and economic realms.[30]

Promotion of care giver equity

The second direction in which socio-economic policy should be encouraged, namely, fostering the entry of potential care givers into caring situations and their continuation in them, involves questions of equity. As has been discussed at various points, the argument for strengthening the position of care givers and acknowledging their social and economic contributions meets here with the need to strengthen, create, and foster the performance of caring services in a large part of society. Since "one cannot rely on the falling-in-love pattern (which involves the giving of a little more than each gets) to raise general levels of benevolence" (Boulding 1978: 203), it has been suggested that one of the most sensible and effective ways of reaching both aims is to reduce the asymmetries and dependencies involved in caring situations induced by societal values and institutions and strengthen the position of care givers in society by promoting *care giver equity*.[31] As shown in the previous chapters, this would mean, among other things, reducing material dependency of care givers by ensuring their adequate access to resources, improving their relative income situation, and

---

[29] On the "importance of options" and on the "importance of perceived worth" see also Nussbaum 2001: 285-288.

[30] Cf. e.g. Biesecker 1996; Jochimsen 2001.

[31] In looking at equity concerns in social welfare a most convincing normative framework comes from Nancy Fraser (Fraser 1997a). Fraser focuses on the notion of "gender equity," conceptualizing it as a compound of seven distinct normative principles: "antipoverty," "antiexploitation," "income equality," "leisure-time equality," "equality of respect," "antimarginalization," and "antiandrocentrism" (Fraser 1997a: 44-49). The vision behind Fraser's gender equity is a "Universal Caregiver Model", viewing individuals as people with the responsibility and task of performing "dependency services. (Fraser 1997a: 51-62) See also Badgett and Folbre 1999; Perrons 2000. For a practical example cf. Brouwer and Wierda 1998 on the Dutch Combination Model.

adequately paying dependency workers. This, in turn, would enlarge the choices for care givers (and care receivers) among alternative dependency situations. Reducing asymmetries and dependencies in caring would also mean ensuring time control for care givers, taking account of the double burden of professional and family life, and allowing room for care givers' self-care. Efforts undertaken against the devaluation of care and dependency work and the discrimination of care givers on the basis of gender, race, class, and ethnicity would lessen the existing asymmetry in recognition between those inside and those outside caring relationships.

Care giver equity could help prevent caring motivations from being taken advantage of and would foster the continuation of motivation in dependency workers. It would also likely be one of the strongest encouragements for the creation of caring motivations in providers (employers, administration, informal providers) and among those individuals who are not involved in immediate dependency relationships. It could thus reverse the crowding-out effect of inadequate working conditions, the material dependency of care givers, the social devaluation of care work, and the discrimination against care givers. A crowding-in effect could well be the result. The promotion of a less discriminating and more equity-oriented change in societal values toward care giving and care receiving would enhance the attractiveness of voluntarily entering into the performance of dependency work.[32]

If societies fail to deal adequately with the coordinates of the social organization of caring situations, if they ignore the sensitive points in the social organization of caring, the most obvious losers will be the most vulnerable: infants and the sick, the disabled, and elderly with existential dependency needs. The lack of an integrative product of caring and the resulting loss, however, have a public dimension that affects all members of society. Careful economics must provide the analytical tools to detect and avoid such situations.

[32] Care giver equity, furthermore, is likely to be a strong argument in legitimizing policy measures if labor grants must be socially organized through mandates. It would also help combat poor working conditions where care workers from abroad are employed illegally and/or without social security benefits.

REFERENCES

Abel, Emily K. and Margaret K. Nelson (eds.). 1990. *Circles of Care. Work and Identity in Women's Lives.* Albany: State University of New York Press.

Abel, Emily K. and Margaret K. Nelson. 1990a. "Circles of Care. An Introductory Essay," in Emily K. Abel and Margaret K. Nelson (eds.) *Circles of Care. Work and Identity in Women's Lives*, pp. 4-34. Albany: State University of New York Press.

Akerlof, George A. 1982. "Labor Contracts as Partial Gift Exchange," *The Quarterly Journal of Economics* 97 (4): 543-569.

Andreas, Heike. 1994. *Problemgeschichte der Gesundheitsökonomik in der Bundesrepublik Deutschland. Die ökonomische Steuerung von Angebot und Nachfrage im Gesundheitswesen von der Kostenexplosion bis zum Gesundheitsstrukturgesetz.* Cologne: Botermann & Botermann.

Andreoni, James. 1989. "Giving with Impure Altruism. Applications to Charity and Ricardian Equivalence," in *Journal of Political Economy* 97: 1447-1458.

Anheier, Helmut K., Eckhard Priller, Wolfgang Seibel and Annette Zimmer (eds.) *Der Dritte Sektor in Deutschland. Organisationen zwischen Staat und Markt im gesellschaftlichen Wandel.* Berlin: edition sigma.

Arrow, Kenneth J. 1972. "Gifts and Exchanges," *Philosophy and Public Affairs* 1 (4): 343-362.

Badgett, Lee and Nancy Folbre. 1999. "Assigning Care: Gender Norms and Economic Outcomes," *International Labour Review* 138 (3): 311-326.

Barker, Drucilla K. and Edith Kuiper (eds.). 2003. *Toward a Feminist Philosophy of Economics.* London and New York: Routledge. *Forthcoming*

Becker, Gary S. 1996. *Accounting for Tastes.* Cambridge MA and London: Harvard University Press.

Becker, Gary S. 1981. *A Treatise on the Family.* Cambridge MA: Harvard University Press.

Becker, Gary S. 1976 (paperback 1978). *The Economic Approach to Human Behavior.* Chicago and London: The University of Chicago Press.

Benería, Lourdes. 1999. "The Enduring Debate over Unpaid Labour," *International Labour Review* 138 (3): 287-309.

Ben-Ner, Avner and Louis Putterman (eds.). 1998. *Economics, Values, and Organization.* Cambridge: Cambridge University Press.

Bergmann, Barbara R. 1995 "Becker's Theory of the Family. Preposterous Conclusions," *Feminist Economics* 1 (1): 141-150.

Biesecker, Adelheid and Klaus Grenzdörffer (eds.). 1996. *Kooperation, Netzwerk, Selbstorganisation – Elemente demokratischen Wirtschaftens.* Pfaffenweiler: Centaurus.

Biesecker, Adelheid. 1996. "Kooperation, Netzwerk, Selbstorganisation – Prinzipien für eine faire und vorsorgende Ökonomie," in Adelheid Biesecker and Klaus Grenzdörffer (eds.) *Kooperation, Netzwerk, Selbstorganisation. Elemente demokratischen Wirtschaftens*, pp. 9-21. Pfaffenweiler: Centaurus.

Blau, Francine D., Marianne A. Ferber, and Anne E. Winkler. 1998 (1986, 1992). *The Economics of Women, Men, and Work.* Third edition. Upper Saddle River NJ: Prentice Hall.

Boulding, Kenneth E. 1978. *Ecodynamics. A New Theory of Societal Evolution.* Beverly Hills and London: Sage Publications.

Boulding, Kenneth E. 1973. *The Economy of Love and Fear. A Preface to Grants Economics.* Belmont CA: Wadsworth.

Bowden, Peta. 1997. *Caring. Gender-sensitive Ethics.* London and New York: Routledge.

Bowers, Barbara. 1990. "Family Perceptions of Care in a Nursing Home," in Emily K. Abel and Margaret K. Nelson (eds.) *Circles of Care. Work and Identity in Women's Lives*, pp. 278-289. Albany: State University of New York Press.

Brodkin Sacks, Karen. 1990. "Does it Pay to Care?," in Emily K. Abel and Margaret K. Nelson (eds.) *Circles of Care. Work and Identity in Women's Lives*, pp. 188-206. Albany: State University of New York Press.

Brouwer, Ina and Eelco Wierda. 1998. "The Combination Model. Child Care and the Part Time Labour Labour Supply of Men in the Dutch Welfare State," in J. J. Schippers, J. J. Siegers and J. de Jong-Gierfeld (eds.) *Child Care and Female Labour Supply in the Netherlands. Facts, Analyses, Policies*, Amsterdam: Thesis Publishers.

Chiappori, Pierre-André. 1988. "Rational Household Labor Supply," *Econometrica* 56 (1): 63-89.

Dahl, Robert A. and Charles E. Lindblom. 1953. *Politics, Economics, and Welfare.* New York: Harper and Brothers.

Diamond, Timothy. 1990. "Nursing Homes as Trouble," in Emily K. Abel and Margaret K. Nelson (eds.) *Circles of Care. Work and Identity in Women's Lives*, pp. 173-187. Albany: State University of New York Press.

Dwyer, Daisy and Judith Bruce (eds.). 1988. *A Home Divided: Women and Income in the Third World.* Stanford: Stanford University Press.

England, Paula. 1993. "The Separative Self. Androcentric Bias in Neoclassical Assumptions," in Marianne A. Ferber and Julie A. Nelson (eds.) *Beyond Economic Man. Feminist Theory and Economics*, pp. 37-53. Chicago and London: University of Chicago Press.

Evers, Adalbert. 2001. "Aktivierender Sozialstaat (II). Ein Beitrag zur Vitalisierung der Bürgergesellschaft?" *Theorie und Praxis der Sozialen Arbeit* 3/2001: 83-89.

Fehr, Ernst and Klaus M. Schmidt. 2000. Theories of Fairness and Reciprocity. Evidence and Economic Applications. CESifo Working Paper Series. Working Paper No. 403. December.

Ferber, Marianne A. and Julie A. Nelson (eds.). 1993. *Beyond Economic Man. Feminist Theory and Economics*, pp. 23-36. Chicago and London: University of Chicago Press.

Ferguson, A. 1989. *Blood at the Root: Motherhood, Sexuality and Male Domination.* London: Unwin Hyman and Pandora Press.

Fisher, Berenice and Joan Tronto. 1990. "Toward a Feminist Theory of Caring," in Emily K. Abel and Margaret K. Nelson (eds.) *Circles of Care. Work and Identity in Women's Lives*, pp. 35-62. Albany: State University of New York Press.

Folbre, Nancy. 1995. "Holding Hands at Midnight. The Paradox of Caring Labor," *Feminist Economics* 1 (1): 73-92.

Folbre, Nancy. 1994. *Who Pays for the Kids? Gender and the Structures of Constraint.* London and New York: Routledge.

Folbre, Nancy. 1988. "The Black Four of Hearts: Toward a New Paradigm of Household Economics," in Daisy Dwyer and Judith Bruce (eds.) *A Home Divided: Women and Income in the Third World.* Stanford: Stanford University Press.

Folbre, Nancy and Julie A. Nelson. 2000. "For Love or Money – Or Both?," *The Journal of Economic Perspectives* 14 (4): 123-140.

Folbre, Nancy and Paula England. 1999. "Who Should Pay For the Kids?," *The Annals of The American Academy of Political and Social Science* 562 (May): 194-207.

Folbre, Nancy and Paula England. 1999a. "The Cost of Caring," *The Annals of the American Academy of Political and Social Science* 561 (January): 39-51 (Special Issue on Emotional Labor in the Service Economy, edited by Ronnie J. Steinberg and Deborah M. Figart).

Folbre, Nancy and Thomas Weisskopf. 1998. "Did Father Know Best? Families, Markets, and the Supply of Caring Labor," in Avner Ben-Ner and Louis Putterman (eds.) *Economics, Values, and Organization*, pp. 171-205. Cambridge: Cambridge University Press.

Fraser, Nancy. 1997. *Justice Interruptus. Critical Reflections on the "Postsocialist" Condition*. New York and London: Routledge.

Fraser, Nancy. 1997a. "After the Family Wage. A Postindustrial Thought Experiment," in Nancy Fraser *Justice Interruptus. Critical Reflections on the "Postsocialist" Condition*, pp. 41-66. New York and London: Routledge.

Fraser, Nancy and Linda Gordon. 1997. "A Genealogy of 'Dependency.' Tracing a Keyword of the U.S. Welfare State," in Nancy Fraser *Justice Interruptus. Critical Reflections on the "Postsocialist" Condition*, pp. 121-149. New York and London: Routledge.

Frey, Bruno S. 1998. "Institutions and Morale. The Crowding-out Effect," in Avner Ben-Ner and Louis Putterman (eds.) *Economics, Values, and Organization*, pp. 437-460. Cambridge: Cambridge University Press.

Frey, Bruno S. 1997. *Not Just For the Money. An Economic Theory of Personal Motivation*. Cheltenham: Edward Elgar.

Frey, Bruno S. 1993. Motivation as a Limit to Pricing. *Journal of Economic Psychology* 14: 635-664.

Gäfgen, Gérard. 1990. *Gesundheitsökonomische Grundlagen und Anwendungen*. Baden-Baden: Nomos.

Gardiner, Jean. 1997. *Gender, Care and Economics*. Houndsmills and London: Macmillan Press.

Gilligan, Carol. 1982. *In a Different Voice. Psychological Theory and Women's Development*. Cambridge MA: Harvard University Press.

Gouldner, Alvin W. 1996 (1960). "The Norm of Reciprocity: A Preliminary Statement," in Aafke E. Komter (ed.) *The Gift. An Interdisciplinary Perspective*, pp. 49-66. Amsterdam: Amsterdam University Press. [From Gouldner, Alvin W. 1960. "The Norm of Reciprocity: A Preliminary Statement," *American Sociological Review* 25 (2): 161-178]

Gustafsson, Siv S. 1994. "Childcare and Types of Welfare States," in Diane Sainsbury (ed.) *Gendering Welfare States*, pp. 45-61. London: Sage Publications.

Gustafsson, Siv S. 1993. Feminist Neoclassical Economics. Tinbergen Institute. Paper 93-255. Amsterdam.

Hawrylyshyn, Oli. 1977. "Towards a Definition of Non-Market Activities," *The Review of Income and Wealth* 23 (1): 79-96.

Held, Virginia. 2002. "Care and the Extension of Markets," *Hypatia. A Journal of Feminist Philosophy* 17 (2): 20-33.

Herder-Dorneich, Philipp. 1980. *Gesundheitsökonomik. Systemsteuerung und Ordnungspolitik im Gesundheitswesen*. Stuttgart: Ferdinand Enke Verlag.

Hill, T.P. 1977. "On Goods and Services," *The Review of Income and Wealth* 23 (4): 315-338.

Himmelweit, Susan. 2002. "Making Visible the Hidden Economy. The Case for Gender-Impact Analysis of Economic Policy," *Feminist Economics* 8 (1): 49-70.

Himmelweit, Susan (ed.). 2000. *Inside the Household. From Labour to Care*. Houndsmills, Basingstoke: Macmillan Press Ltd.

Himmelweit, Susan. 1999. "Caring Labor," *The Annals of the American Academy of Political and Social Science* 561 (January): 27-38 (Special Issue on Emotional Labor in the Service Economy, edited by Ronnie J. Steinberg and Deborah M. Figart).

Himmelweit, Susan. 1997. Why Do We Care about Caring? Paper presented at the ASSA meetings, New Orleans, January 4-6.

Himmelweit, Susan. 1996. Conceptualizing Caring. Paper presented at the International Association for Feminist Economics Conference, Washington DC, July.

Himmelweit, Susan. 1995. "The Discovery of 'Unpaid Work.' The Social Consequences of the Expansion of 'Work,'" *Feminist Economics* 1 (1): 1-19.

Hirschman, Albert O. 1970. *Exit, Voice, and Loyalty. Responses to Decline in Firms, Organizations, and State.* Cambridge MA and London: Harvard University Press.

Hochschild, Arlie Russell. 1983. *The Managed Heart. Commercialization of Human Feeling.* Berkeley, Los Angeles, London: University of California Press.

Hodgson, Geoffrey. 1988 (1989, 1993). *Economics and Institutions. A Manifesto for a Modern Institutional Economics.* Cambridge: Polity Press.

Hoskins, Irene. 1993. "Combining Work and Care for the Elderly: An Overview of the Issues," *International Labour Review* 132 (3): 347-369.

Jochimsen, Maren A. 2003. "Integrating Vulnerability. On the Impact of Caring on Economic Theorizing," in Drucilla K. Barker and Edith Kuiper (eds.) *Toward a Feminist Philosophy of Economics*, London and New York: Routledge. *Forthcoming*

Jochimsen, Maren A. 2003a. "Die Gestaltungskraft des Asymmetrischen. Kennzeichen klassischer Sorgesituationen und ihre theoretische Erfassung in der Ökonomik," *zfwu – Journal for Business, Economics & Ethics* 4 (1). *Forthcoming*

Jochimsen, Maren A. 2001. Kooperation im Umgang mit Verletzlichkeit. Eckpunkte der Organisation von Sorgesituationen in der Ökonomie. Paper presented at the Annual Conference of the Institute for Institutional and Socio-Economics, University of Bremen. February 23.

Jochimsen, Maren A. 1998. Towards a Concept of Caring Activities (1). Paper presented at the Political Economy Seminar at Harvard University. March 31.

Jochimsen, Maren A. 1998a. Towards a Concept of Caring Activities (2). Paper presented at the Belle van Zuylen Institute, University of Amsterdam. December 4.

Jochimsen, Maren A. 1994. *Die Poetisierung der Ökonomie. Novalis' Thesen im 'Heinrich von Ofterdingen' als Ansatzpunkte für eine ökologieorientierte Ökonomie.* Stuttgart: Verlag Heinz.

Jochimsen, Maren A. and Ulrike Knobloch. 1997 "Making the Hidden Visible. The Importance of Caring Activities and Their Principles for Any Economy," *Ecological Economics* 20 (29): 107-112.

Jochimsen, Maren A. and Ulrike Knobloch. 1993. Towards a Caring Economy. Broadening the Economic Method from an Ethical Perspective. Paper presented at the Conference Out of the Margin. Feminist Perspectives on Economic Theory, Amsterdam, June.

Kirchgässner, Gebhard. 2000. *Homo Oeconomicus. Das ökonomische Modell individuellen Verhaltens und seine Anwendung in den Wirtschafts- und Sozialwissenschaften.* 2nd revised and enlarged edition. Tübingen: J.C.B. Mohr.

Kirchgässner, Gebhard. 1997. Auf der Suche nach dem Gespenst des Ökonomismus. University of St. Gallen, Department of Economics, Discussion Paper No. 9703, April.

Kirchgässner, Gebhard. 1996. "Bemerkungen zur Minimalmoral," *Zeitschrift für Wirtschafts- und Sozialwissenschaften* 116 (2): 223-251.

Kittay, Eva F. 1999. *Love's Labor. Essays on Women, Equality, and Dependency.* New York and London: Routledge.

Kittay, Eva F. and Ellen K. Feder. 2003. *The Subject of Care. Feminist Perspectives on Dependency.* Lanhan: Rowman & Littlefield.

Komter, Aafke E. (ed.). 1996. *The Gift. An Interdisciplinary Perspective.* Amsterdam: Amsterdam University Press.

Komter, Aafke E. 1996a. "Women, Gifts, and Power," in Aafke E. Komter (ed.) *The Gift. An Interdisciplinary Perspective*, pp. 119-131. Amsterdam: Amsterdam University Press.

Levison, Deborah. 2000. "Children as Economic Agents," *Feminist Economics* 6 (1): 125-134 (Special Issue on Children and Family Policy, guest-edited by Nancy Folbre and Susan Himmelweit).

Macdonald, Cameron Lynne and Carmen Sirianni (eds.). 1996. *Working in the Service Society*. Philadelphia: Temple University Press.

Macdonald, Cameron Lynne and Carmen Sirianni. 1996a. "The Service Society and the Changing Experience of Work," in Cameron Lynne Macdonald and Carmen Sirianni (eds.) *Working in the Service Society*, pp. 1-26. Philadelphia: Temple University Press.

Malinowski, Bronislaw. 1996. "The Principle of Give and Take," in Aafke E. Komter (ed.) *The Gift. An Interdisciplinary Perspective*, pp. 15-17. Amsterdam: Amsterdam University Press. [From Malinowski, Bronislaw. 1970 (1922). *Crime and Custom in Savage Society*, pp. 39-40. London: Routledge and Kegan Paul]

Manser, Marilyn and Murray Brown. 1980. "Marriage and Household Decision-Making: A Bargaining Analysis," *International Economic Review* 21: 31-44.

McCrate, Elaine. 1987. "Trade, Merger and Employment. Economic Theory on Marriage," *Review of Radical Political Economics* 19 (1): 73-89.

Nelson, Julie A. 2001. Why Are Early Education and Care Wages so Low? A Critical Guide to Common Explanations, Foundation for Child Development Working Paper Series, April.

Nelson, Julie A. 1999. "Of Markets and Martyrs. Is It Ok To Pay Well For Care?," *Feminist Economics* 5 (3): 43-59.

Nelson, Julie A. 1998. For Love or Money – or Both? Paper presented at the International Association for Feminist Economics /Out of the Margin 2 Conference, Amsterdam, 2-6 June, revised July.

Nelson, Julie A. 1996. *Feminism, Objectivity, and Economics*. London: Routledge.

Nelson, Julie A. 1993. "The Study of Choice or the Study of Provisioning? Gender and the Definition of Economics," in Marianne A. Ferber and Julie A. Nelson (eds.) *Beyond Economic Man. Feminist Theory and Economics*, pp. 23-36. Chicago and London: University of Chicago Press.

Nelson, Julie A. 1992. "The Study of Choice or the Study of Provisioning? Gender and the Definition of Economics," in Marianne A. Ferber and Julie A. Nelson (eds.) *Beyond Economic Man. Feminist Theory and Economics*, pp. 23-36. Chicago and London: University of Chicago Press.

Nelson, Julie A. and Paula England. 2002. "Feminist Philosophies of Love and Work," *Hypatia. A Journal of Feminist Philosophy* 17 (2): 1-18.

Nelson, Margaret K. 1990. "Mothering Other's Children. The Experiences of Family Day Care Providers," in Emily K. Abel and Margaret K. Nelson (eds.) *Circles of Care. Work and Identity in Women's Lives*, pp. 210-232. Albany: State University of New York Press.

Noddings, Nel. 1984. *Caring. A Feminine Approach to Ethics and Moral Education*. Berkeley CA: University of California Press.

Nussbaum, Martha C. 2001 (2000). *Women and Human Development. The Capabilities Approach*. First paperback edition. Cambridge: Cambridge University Press.

Nussbaum, Martha C. 1999. *Sex and Social Justice*. Oxford et al.: Oxford University Press.

Ottnad, Adrian. 2000. "Die Rolle der Freien Wohlfahrtspflege in der Sozialen Marktwirtschaft," in *Sozialer Fortschritt. Unabhängige Zeitung für Sozialpolitik* 11-12/2000: 270-278.

Ottnad, Adrian. 2000a. "Die Freie Wohlfahrtpflege am Scheideweg. Der Markt für soziale Dienstleistungen steht vor grundlegenden Veränderungen," in *WiSt* 8/2000: 473-475.

Ottnad, Adrian, Stefanie Wahl and Meinhard Miegel. 2000. *Zwischen Markt und Mildtätigkeit. Die Bedeutung der Freien Wohlfahrtspflege für Gesellschaft, Wirtschaft und Beschäftigung.* (A study of the Institut for Economy and Society (IWG) Bonn). München: Olzog.

Perrons, Diane. 2000. "Care, Paid Work, and Leisure. Rounding the Triangle," *Feminist Economics* 6 (1): 105-114 (Special Issue on Children and Family Policy, guest-edited by Nancy Folbre and Susan Himmelweit).

Plantenga, Janneke. 1998. The Economics of a Female Friendly Welfare State. The Case of Child Care Services In Sweden and the Netherlands. Paper presented at the International Association for Feminist Economics /Out of the Margin 2 Conference, Amsterdam, 2-6 June.

Plantenga, Janneke. 1998a. Care Arrangements in Europe and Brussels Policy. Paper prepared for the Seminar on European Feminist Economics, Brussels, 27-29 November.

Plantenga, Janneke and Marieke J. Sloep. 1995. *Accounting for Unpaid Labour. A Study on the Integration of Unpaid Labour in Macroeconomics Concepts and Models.* Commissioned by the Emancipation Council. The Hague, May (OR 08 -ER/IV 1995).

Pollak, Robert A. 1985. "A Transaction Cost Approach to Families and Households," *Journal of Economic Literature* 23: 581-608.

Putnam, Robert D. 2000. *Bowling Alone. The Collapse and Revival of American Community.* New York et al.: Simon & Schuster.

Putnam, Robert D. 1995. "Bowling Alone. America's Declining Social Capital," *Journal of Democracy* 6 (1): 65-78.

Radin, Margaret Jane. 1996. *Contested Commodities.* Cambridge MA: Harvard University Press.

Reid, Margaret G. 1934. *Economics of Household Production.* New York: John Wiley & Sons; London: Chapman & Hall.

Rifkin, Jeremy. 1995. *The End of Work. The Decline of the Global Labor Force and the Dawn of the Post-Market Era.* New York: (Tarcher) Putnam.

Ruddick, Sarah. 1989. *Maternal Thinking. Towards a Politics of Peace.* Boston: Beacon Press.

Sahlins, Marshall. 1974 (1972). "On the Sociology of Primitive Exchange," in Marshall Sahlins *Stone Age Economics*, pp. 185-275. London: Tavistock Publications.

Schubert, Renate. 1993. *Ökonomische Diskriminierung von Frauen. Eine volkswirtschaftliche Verschwendung.* Frankfurt a.M.: Fischer.

Sen, Amartya K. 1997 (1977). "Rational Fools. A Critique of the Behavioural Foundations of Economic Theory," in Amartya K. Sen *Choice, Welfare and Measurement*, pp. 84-106. [First published in *Philosophy and Public Affairs* 6 (Summer 1977): 317-344] Cambridge MA: Harvard University Press.

Sen, Amartya K. 1997a (1982). *Choice, Welfare and Measurement.* Cambridge MA: Harvard University Press. [First Harvard University Press paperback edition; originally published: Oxford: Blackwell 1982]

Sen, Amartya. 1987. *On Ethics and Economics.* The Royer Lectures. Oxford: Basil Blackwell.

Sen, Amartya. 1985. "Well-being, Agency and Freedom. The Dewey Lectures 1984," *Journal of Philosophy* 82, pp. 169-221.

Sen, Amartya K. 1973. "Behaviour and the Concept of Preference," *Economica* 40: 241-259. (also in Sen 1997a)

Sevenhuijsen, Selma. 1998 (1996). *Citizenship and the Ethics of Care. Feminist Considerations on Justice, Morality and Politics.* London and New York: Routledge.

Soziale Pflegeversicherung mit Nebenbestimmungen. SGB XI. 1996. Second edition. Munich: dtv.

Strassmann, Diana L. 1993a. "The Stories of Economics and the Power of the Storyteller," *History of Political Economy* 25 (1): 147-165.

Strassmann, Diana L. 1993b. "Not a Free Market. The Rhetoric of Disciplinary Authority in Economics," in Marianne A. Ferber and Julie A. Nelson (eds.) *Beyond Economic Man. Feminist Theory and Economics*, pp. 54-68. Chicago and London: University of Chicago Press.

Steinberg, Ronnie and Deborah M. Figart. 1999. "Emotional Labor Since *The Managed Heart*," *The Annals of the American Academy of Political and Social Science* 561 (January): 8-26 (Special Issue on Emotional Labor in the Service Economy, edited by Ronnie J. Steinberg and Deborah M. Figart).

Titmuss, Richard M. 1970. *The Gift Relationship. From Human Blood to Social Policy*. London: George Allen & Unwin Ltd.

Tronto, Joan C. 1993. *Moral Boundaries. A Political Argument for an Ethic of Care*. New York and London: Routledge.

Ulrich, Peter. 1997. *Integrative Wirtschaftsethik. Grundlagen einer lebensdienlichen Ökonomie*. Bern, Stuttgart and Vienna: Haupt.

van Staveren, Irene. 1999. *Caring for Economics. An Aristotelian Perspective*. Delft: Eburon.

Waerness, Kari. 1984. "Caring as Women's Work in the Welfare State," in Holter, H. (ed.) *Patriarchy in a Welfare Society*, pp. 67-87. Oslo: Universitetsforlaget.

Wood, Cynthia A. 1997. "The First World/Third Party Criterion. A Feminist Critique of Production Boundaries in Economics," *Feminist Economics* 3 (3): 47-68.

Zimmer, Annette and Eckhard Priller. 1997. "Zukunft des Dritten Sektors in Deutschland," in Helmut K. Anheier, Eckhard Priller, Wolfgang Seibel and Annette Zimmer (eds.) *Der Dritte Sektor in Deutschland. Organisationen zwischen Staat und Markt im gesellschaftlichen Wandel*, pp. 249-283. Berlin: edition sigma.

INDEX

G

H

I

J

K

L

M

N

O

P

GPSR Compliance

The European Union's (EU) General Product Safety Regulation (GPSR) is a set of rules that requires consumer products to be safe and our obligations to ensure this.

If you have any concerns about our products, you can contact us on ProductSafety@springernature.com

In case Publisher is established outside the EU, the EU authorized representative is:

Springer Nature Customer Service Center GmbH
Europaplatz 3
69115 Heidelberg, Germany

Batch number: 10844692

Printed by Printforce, the Netherlands